extreme

Prayer

MAKEOVER

JOE CAMENETI

extreme Prayer MAKEOVER

REMODELING LIVES
THROUGH PRAYER

Extreme Prayer Makeover
Remodeling Lives through Prayer

Joseph Cameneti Ministries
P.O. Box 1949
Warren, OH 44482
1.877.330.3341
Web site: www.pastorjoe.com

Published by HonorNet
PO Box 910
Sapulpa, OK 74067
Web site: honornet.net

DEDICATION

THIS BOOK IS DEDICATED TO GOD HIMSELF! When I was a nineteen-year-old boy, He invaded my life with His light and love, giving me hope, joy, and peace—something this world could not offer me. Then He opened my eyes to biblical truths that have allowed me to understand life-changing principles. I now understand why all of heaven sings His praises! Thank You, Father God and Jesus, for teaching me to pray and for giving me a system of prayer that has changed my life forever!

CONTENTS

FOREWORD

*E*VERY ONE OF US *NEEDS* A BOOK LIKE THIS ONE! After all, what is a life with God if it is without effective prayer?—very simply, a relationship starved of intimacy and a journey without direction.

Every believer *knows* that prayer is key…that prayer changes things…that the Creator himself yearns for this exchange with His children. We long to sit in the Father's lap and whisper the things buried deep in our hearts. We love to hear His voice leading us, loving us, and empowering us. Yet we are familiar with the challenges pray-ers face—the times when what to pray is uncertain, when results are lagging, when the heart is at a loss for words, and the schedule screams for us to set aside prayer till later.

God knows about the challenges too. I believe that He has filled Pastor Cameneti's heart to overflowing with creative and practical ways to approach prayer—and overcome the obstacles. In a clear and detailed manner, Pastor Cameneti shares those "God ideas" with us. I'm thrilled

at all it will mean to people like you and me—readers all
over the world whose prayer lives will be invigorated, and
whose destinies will be transformed…to impact eternity!

—*Marilyn Hickey*

INTRODUCTION

Remodeling Lives through Prayer

PRAYER. THIS WORD IS FAMILIAR TO MOST everyone, and vast numbers of people around the world practice it in their lives. But did you know that prayer is the most powerful weapon on earth? It is true. Prayer is the vehicle that releases God to move in the lives of people here on earth. When you understand how to pray and what to pray for, you can watch God remodel you—and those for whom you pray—from the inside out!

This book was birthed out of great frustration in my own prayer life. I was a Bible college graduate, and was senior pastor of a wonderful church where I had served for more than twenty years. I had attended seminar after seminar on the subject of prayer, taught by some of the best teachers in the world. Yet something seemed to be missing in my prayer life. Like many others who have prayed a certain way for so long that prayer has become commonplace, I found that my prayers were hit and miss—not consistently effective.

I longed to have a more powerful prayer life. I wanted to pray more effective prayers—prayers that caused things to change…prayers that produced results. As I began to seek God for truth and guidance about prayer, He began to reveal to me exciting information that has changed my life.

The information I share in this book may be one of the most unique and exciting revelations about praying effective, Bible-based prayers that you have ever seen. In chapter one, you will discover how God changed my prayer life forever as a result of His supernatural revelation about the *Remodel Prayer Card System*. I'm so thankful that I now know how to pray prayers that get results—changing not only my life, but also the lives of the people for whom I pray.

I am excited about sharing this prayer system with you. So get ready to have your prayer life remodeled forever…and get ready to see wonderful changes in the lives of the people for whom you pray!

1

The Day God Changed My Prayer Life!

EVERAL YEARS AGO, I SAT WITH MY WIFE, Gina, and our two daughters and watched a television program called "Extreme Makeover: Home Edition." I had never seen it before, and I found it to be a refreshing change from most of the other viewing options. The program offers heartwarming stories about caring people helping people in need.

Applications recommending someone who desperately needs a home renovation, but can't afford it because of tragic accidents, severe handicaps, or serious illnesses, are submitted to program officials by someone who knows of their need. Out of those applications, a family is chosen to be the recipient of a total home makeover.

The surprised and grateful recipients are provided comfortable accommodations elsewhere while the total makeover of their home is being done. And it is a *total* makeover—no little patch-up jobs or shoddy material and workmanship—but the best of the best, including furniture and interior decorating.

When the project is finally done, the fortunate family returns for the surprise of their lives, accompanied by tears of joy and inadequate words to express their gratitude. The entire process is captured on film and presented on television, a very appealing and heartwarming story. I really enjoyed watching the program, and I caught myself thinking about it from time to time.

A DIVINE CONNECTION

I had become increasingly frustrated with my prayer life. I felt that my prayers for other people were hit and miss at best, and I sensed that there must be a better and more effective way to do it. Surely there must be some method I could follow to ensure that I was praying everything according to the Bible and that I didn't forget to pray for something important.

Now, as a long-time Christian and minister, I had heard a lot of teaching on the subject of prayer, and I had studied the Bible and preached on prayer many times. I could find all the scriptures on what to pray for Christians, but it took a long time, and I felt that there ought to be some way to organize them so they would be easier to utilize.

Several months later, as I was praying and confessing my frustration about the matter, all of a sudden "Extreme Makeover: Home Edition" popped into my mind. Although I didn't realize it at the time, I believe this was a divine connection. As I continued to pray, curious about that sudden thought, the word "remodel" came to mind. Then I began to see it as an acronym, and appropriate words for each of the seven letters started coming to me. I always have a paper and pen with me when I pray, so I began writing down the thoughts as they came to me. When I was finished, this is what I had:

R—Rescue from Evil

E—Expanded Love

M—More Boldness

O—Open Eyes

D—Deeper Desire

E—Extra Strength

L—Lord's Will and Wisdom

Then I searched out all the scriptures about praying for others, and began to put them in one of the seven categories. When I was finished, every scripture had fit perfectly in one of the categories. I was amazed when I realized there were seven letters in the acronym and that all the scriptures fit in so well.

If you study numbers in the Bible, seven is the number for perfection or completion. The word *REMODEL* has seven letters, which represent seven areas of prayer—important areas that will bring perfection and completeness into the lives of those for whom you pray.

All of this was so exciting—I wondered if it could be the answer to my prayers. I couldn't wait to use it as a guide during my prayer time.

GOD'S PART...MY PART

For several months, I used the words and scriptures as I prayed, adding and changing things along the way. As I continued using the *REMODEL* notes and scriptures when I prayed, I soon realized that my prayers were no longer "hit and miss," but consistently thorough and powerful. I also discovered that this exciting new method could be adapted for two versions—a short version to use when time is limited and a longer version to use when you have more time.

CHANGING A PERSON'S WILL IS GOD'S JOB.

I found that by memorizing the *R-E-M-O-D-E-L* acronym, I could pray three- to five-minute prayers while taking a shower or driving in my car. In that brief time, I was able to pray for someone, covering all seven areas.

Then when time permitted or I felt a greater unction or urge to pray for someone, I could spend more time praying about the seven specific areas more thoroughly.

Through the process, I learned an important lesson. Although I couldn't change people and cause them to do right, I began to realize that my prayers were releasing the Holy Spirit to move in their lives, changing them from the inside out…giving them different desires.

I began to see that changing a person's will is God's job. In Philippians, the apostle Paul says:

> …it is God Who is all the while effectually at work in you [energizing and creating in you the power and desire], both to will and to work for His good pleasure and satisfaction and delight.
>
> —Philippians 2:13 AMP

Only God can change people's desires, but we have the responsibility of praying and releasing Him to move in their lives.

As Christians, we have an awesome responsibility—one that must not be taken lightly—and we must depend on the powerful vehicle of prayer to help us effectively accomplish God's perfect plan in the earth. We have been given a great place of authority in the earth, and we must be careful to acknowledge our sovereign God and seek His guidance in prayer to properly fulfill our roles. When I realized the authority that God had entrusted to me, it made me want to pray all the more.

We must understand that God's will isn't always going to be done on earth unless we pray. There are some people who are not mature enough to pray for themselves, and unless someone else prays His will into their lives, it won't happen. It is a sobering thought to realize that there are people who may never walk in the will of God unless we pray His will into their lives. God has given us the keys and the authority to pray His will into their lives, and that's why we must pray.

> GOD HAS GIVEN US THE RESPONSIBILITY AND THE RIGHT TO LOOSE HIS POWER AND HIS WILL INTO THE LIVES OF BOTH THE UNSAVED AND THE SAVED.

It is exciting to know that no situation is hopeless when we are faithful to do our part by praying God's will into the earth and into individual lives. Jesus says in Luke 18:1 *"...that men always ought to pray and not lose heart"* (NKJV). This means that no matter how difficult the person or situation, we can pray and bring the kingdom of God—the presence of God—on the scene. We can pray and witness the very will of God moving into the hearts and lives of those for whom we pray.

God has given us the responsibility and the right to loose His power and His will into the lives of both the unsaved and the saved. We can also pray and release His will into difficult situations. The Bible is full of great examples in the book of Acts. When people prayed according to God's will, He was released into difficult situations and great things happened. Those prayer warriors were no different than you and me today—we can have effective prayer lives just like they had. We can pray and see powerful results.

I believe there has been a tendency in the past several years for people to overemphasize praying against the devil instead of praying for the release of God. There are times when we must come against the devil, but when the Bible deals with prayer, it is generally directed toward releasing God's kingdom and will into the world. I believe we must be careful to put the emphasis where it belongs.

PRAY LIGHT INTO DARKNESS

In the book of Acts, when the saints were attacked or persecuted, they prayed for the kingdom of God to come—for God to show up. And when God showed up, freedom came. Acts, chapter four, is a great example to study sometime. It is no different for us today—when we pray, God shows up…and when He does, the kingdom of darkness shakes. Light always overcomes darkness. We shouldn't be so concerned about the darkness of the world, because by praying that the kingdom of heaven will come and that God's will be done, we are bringing light and power to the world. And His light and power will change people, families, and situations. Nothing will change a person quicker than getting the life of God flowing into

GOD HAS GIVEN US THE KEYS TO HIS KINGDOM, AND IT IS OUR PRIVILEGE AND RESPONSIBILITY TO USE THEM.

their lives. So when we pray the light and power—God's will—into the world, darkness has to go. Light, life, and the power of God can be released into our lives, homes, cities, and governments when we praise God and pray His will.

When we see Christian brothers or sisters who seem to be losing the intimate relationships and trust they once had with God, we need to pray on their behalf. No person or situation is hopeless, and it is our responsibility to pray that God will bring about the change that is His will for their lives. God has given us the keys to His kingdom, and it is our privilege and responsibility to use them.

UNLOCK GOD'S WILL FOR MARRIAGES

I remember one man in our church who experienced such great disappointment in his wife that he left her and didn't want to have anything to do with her. His mind was made up and that was just the way he wanted it to be. But as his Christian brothers and sisters began to pray for God's will to come into his life, God got involved and touched his life. The man began to feel drawn to his wife, and as we continued to pray, God brought them back together and restored their marriage.

If you are experiencing problems in your marriage, you must understand that it is not hopeless. No matter what you have done or what your mate has done, God can bring about change. Instead of complaining, arguing, and fighting, use the keys—pray for God's will to be done in your marriage relationship.

It is one of the most wonderful feelings in the world to know that you have at least one person praying for you. In all the years that Gina and I have been married, she has never torn me down. But I know one thing that she is doing—she is praying for me. And I pray for her too. When I know that she is struggling with a particular situation, I pray for her every day. I encourage you to read on and learn how powerful prayer is and how you can use the R-E-M-O-D-E-L prayer system as you pray for your marriage, your spouse, and everyone you love and care about. No matter what is going on, positive changes can come about when we pray and unlock God's will in our situation.

> DON'T EVER GIVE UP, THINKING THAT A PERSON OR SITUATION IS HOPELESS.

DON'T GIVE UP—THERE IS ALWAYS HOPE

Don't ever give up, thinking that a person or situation is hopeless. When you can pray, there is always hope. Sometimes we see Christians who don't seem to be maturing spiritually—in fact, it appears that they are so carnal and messed up that even God can't fix them, but that isn't true. We must realize that the more they mess up, the more prayer they need. If they haven't changed and they seem hopeless, it may be because we're not praying for them and releasing God's will in their lives. The apostle Paul prayed for believers more than anything else. He prayed that God would be released and get involved in their lives. I believe this should motivate us to be diligent in praying more effectively so that our own lives and the lives of others can be changed.

In Colossians 4, Paul says to the church at Colossi:

> *Epaphras, who is one of you and a servant of Christ Jesus, sends greetings. He is always wrestling in prayer for you, that you may stand firm in all the will of God, mature and fully assured.*
> —Colossians 4:12

Paul wanted the Christians at Colossi to know that Epaphras was *always* praying for them. He didn't give up on them. He was a prayer warrior who wrestled in prayer, praying God's will for them consistently. He prayed first of all that they would stand firm in the will of God—that God's will for their lives would be accomplished. Then he prayed that they would mature spiritually. Think about what a blessing that must have been to those Christians—to know that someone was fervently, consistently praying God's will for their lives.

Our consistent prayers for God's will to be done in the lives of individuals who are out of step with God's plan will get results, but sometimes it takes a long time. A lady in our church told me that she had witnessed to and prayed for a woman for ten years. The woman came to church several times, and finally one week—after all those years—she responded and accepted Christ as her Savior. Just a short time later, the woman died. What if our church member had decided that the woman was a hopeless case and quit praying for her? I'm telling you, it is our privilege to pray for others, but more than that it is an awesome responsibility that God has entrusted to us.

GET READY FOR THE GREAT ADVENTURE!

This walk with Jesus is an exciting adventure, and I love it. I'm not a person who enjoys sitting still very long, so I enjoy the excitement of walking with God. Life is a big adventure with all kinds of things happening, and I have the privilege and ability to pray and then watch someone's life change for the better—to pray and release the power of God into someone's life and watch Him do something great. I have endeavored in my life to follow Paul's example—to pray without ceasing. That doesn't mean that I pray every minute of the day—it simply means that I have a consistent prayer life. You, too, can enjoy the great adventure of consistently praying prayers that make a difference—prayers that get results and change lives.

You will find more information about the *Remodel Prayer Card System* in other chapters of this book.

Pastor Joe's Main Points Review

1. Using the R-E-M-O-D-E-L acronym, thorough and effective three- to five-minute prayers can be prayed for anyone.

2. Only God can change people, but He can use your prayers to release the Holy Spirit to move in their lives, changing them from the inside out.

3. You can pray and witness the very will of God moving into the hearts and lives of those for whom you pray.

4. When you pray, there is always hope.

2

Why Do You Pray?

THIS IS AN INTERESTING AND THOUGHT-provoking question—one you may not have considered. Most of us would probably say that we pray because we need God to help us with a particular problem or need. Most of us also believe—or want to believe—that God will answer our prayers. But there is more you need to know about prayer.

God's position on prayer is very clear in His Word:

This is the confidence we have in approaching God: that if we ask anything according to his will, he hears us. And if we know that he hears us—whatever we ask—we know that we have what we asked of him.

—1 John 5:14,15

15

This verse clearly says we can pray with confidence, knowing that God *will* answer our prayers *if* we pray according to His will. Studying the Bible for ourselves helps us understand the truth, which is that there's only one contingency to getting what we ask for—asking according to God's will. This means that it is very important to be informed about the will of God.

Some have misinterpreted these verses, saying that God only answers our prayers based on whether He wants to or not. They say that His will is what He wants to do at a particular time. It is true that God is sovereign—He knows what is best for each one of us, and He gives to us according to what is in our best interest...according to His will. I'm sure you have heard many people pray, "Oh Lord, if it be Thy will, please give me this." And certainly there are times when praying, "Not my will, but Your will be done" is appropriate. That is the prayer Jesus prayed in the Garden of Gethsemane concerning the cup of suffering. The human part of Jesus wanted to bypass going to the cross if possible, but ultimately He trusted His Father's plan and chose to put His life in God's hands.

All of us should pray this prayer of consecration every morning, asking God to be in control of what happens in our everyday lives. When we face situations that require a decision to do one thing or another and we are unsure of what to do, we must trust God and ask Him to give us direction. But that is not the same as praying for something that has already been settled—something that is written in the Word of God.

God's Word in verse 14 represents the will of God—His declared will for His children. It is imperative that we know and understand His will for us concerning prayer if we are to have confidence when we pray. Once we know what the Bible says on the subject, we can have confidence that every time we enter the throne room and present our petitions according to His will, it will be done.

God even has a will concerning *what* we should pray for and *how* we should pray. When we really believe that God will answer our prayers, then we will be stirred up and wanting to pray! The reason we spend time studying the Bible is so we can learn the will of God and be able to pray prayers that God will answer! The *Remodel Prayer Card System* will categorize all the prayers that the Bible says are God's will for you and me to pray for other people—prayers that will release Him to move in their lives!

PRAYER IS NOT A FRUITLESS EXERCISE THAT GOD ASKS US TO PERFORM TO DETERMINE WHETHER OR NOT WE ARE FAITHFUL—PRAYER IS THE VEHICLE THAT RELEASES GOD TO MOVE ON THE EARTH.

God wants you to pray prayers that get results, and the first question you must answer is "Why do I pray?" There are many kinds of prayers and many reasons for praying, and determining why and how you pray can be an eye-opening experience. Do you pray because you think God will be mad at you if you don't? Do you pray because you think you have to in order to be a faithful and mature saint? That kind of motivation may work for a little while, but before long, praying with that kind of an attitude becomes too difficult to continue.

But when you understand what your prayers can do and the effect they can have in the earth, then your prayers will have life, and you will have a greater desire to pray. The insight that God has given me about prayer has totally revolutionized my prayer life, and I believe it will do the same for you. Here is the foundation in one sentence: *Prayer is not a fruitless exercise that God asks us to perform to determine whether or not we are faithful—prayer is the vehicle that releases God to move on the earth.* When you really get hold of that, it will change your life…and the lives of those for whom you pray.

It is wonderful to know that prayer is not just a job God gives us to do to prove ourselves, but a marvelous privilege that brings His will to pass in the earth. It is exciting to realize the necessity of our prayers in partnering with God to see His will accomplished in the earth.

THE KEYS TO THE KINGDOM

You may be wondering, *Exactly how can the way I pray release God to accomplish His will on earth?* Jesus provides the answer:

"I will give you the keys of the kingdom of heaven; whatever you bind on earth will be bound in heaven, and whatever you loose on earth will be loosed in heaven."

—Matthew 16:19

This verse mentions two places. The unseen realm is the kingdom of heaven where God lives. It is the supernatural realm, and we can't see it with our natural eyes, but by faith, we know it is there because the Bible tells us it exists. There is also the natural realm, which is the earth where we live.

This verse provides two important points. First it tells us that even though we cannot see into the heavenly realm, Jesus has given us the keys to the supernatural realm of heaven. These keys give us access to the wonders of the spiritual realm. We have been entrusted with the keys to the realm where God and His power reside and where true life emanates to the natural realm.

Then we are told that by using these keys, whatever we bind on earth will be bound in heaven, and whatever we loose on earth will be loosed in heaven. In the Greek, the two phrases, "bound in heaven" and "loosed in heaven" are in the perfect passive tense, indicating that they are in the state of having already been done. I believe *The Amplified Bible* brings this out more clearly.

> *I will give you the keys of the kingdom of heaven;*
> *and whatever you bind (declare to be improper and*
> *unlawful) on earth must be what is already bound in*
> *heaven; and whatever you loose (declare lawful) on*
> *earth must be what is already loosed in heaven.*
> —Matthew 16:19 AMP

Notice the difference? The most accurate interpretation of this particular passage says that in heaven, the unseen spirit realm, God has already bound and loosed certain things.

Now, since we are in the natural realm, here on earth, we don't see what God has bound and loosed. And unless you have studied the Bible, that may be frustrating and confusing. Some people know that the Bible says we are healed, but when they don't see healing come to pass, they get confused. You must understand that without a doubt, healing has been loosed in the heavenly realm. The Bible says that by the stripes Jesus took on His back, we *were* healed. It has already been declared—it's a done deal! So we can pray for healing with confidence. When we talk to our Father about healing, we know that He hears us because He said it belongs to us. You have the keys to bring it into the natural realm, but until you use the keys, it stays in the heavenly realm, instead of coming to earth.

God has already bound and loosed some things in heaven, and He has given us the keys to bring them to earth. Now, that's something to get excited about. He says, "Here are the keys to heaven, and I want you to use these keys to bind and loose." It is important to understand that the keys will only work when we bind or loose those things that are already bound or loosed in heaven, and we can find information about what those things are in God's Word.

> WHEN WE PRAY, WE CAN LOOSE THE WARMTH AND COMFORT OF ALL OF HEAVEN INTO THE LIVES OF MANY PEOPLE.

Another important point is that when we have the keys, we have the awesome responsibility of control. If you have the keys to a building, you control who can enter that building. If you don't open the door, no one can come in and enjoy the warmth and comfort of the building. So it is with the keys to the kingdom of heaven. When we pray, we can loose the warmth and comfort of all of heaven into the lives of many people. Of course, you're not the only one who has the keys—they are given to all Christians, and we are in control of bringing things out of that realm into the earthly realm. Jesus didn't take the keys to heaven with Him—He left the keys down here with "the church."

Sometimes when we need help, we may say, "God, get those keys and do something." And God would say, "Read the Bible, and you'll discover that I've given *you* the keys, and it is *your* responsibility to use them to do something." We have been given the control, the authority, and we are the ones who determine what comes out of the unseen realm into the earth. If heaven has declared or loosed it, then we have the right to loose it down here. If heaven has said it's not good and it is bound, then we have the right to bind it on earth.

It is an awesome responsibility that we need to recognize. We have the keys and we are in control. We determine what comes out of the heavenly realm and what does not. If we don't do something with what God has given us, then nothing gets done. To put it another way—which may shock you at first—God isn't going to do something until we loose Him to do it by praying His will! If we misunderstand the will of God and sit back, saying, "If He wants to do it, He will do it," then nothing is going to happen. Prayer is using the keys to loose what is in the unseen realm and bring it to the earth.

WHAT A PRIVILEGE WE HAVE TO PARTNER WITH GOD IN PRAYER TO LOOSE HIS WILL ON EARTH.

So why do we pray? We must pray in order to loose the will of God in the earth. God has given us that privilege and responsibility, and if we don't pray, God is not going to move. But when we pray and loose that which has already been loosed in heaven, God is released to send it to the earth. What a privilege we have to partner with God in prayer to loose His will on earth.

Perhaps you're wondering, *Are you saying that we determine what God does or doesn't do?* The answer is yes, and it is based on this scripture. There are others, but this one is, without a doubt, the key scripture that you must get hold of and understand. God is waiting for His people to loose the things that He has already loosed. He's waiting for us to use the keys He has given to us.

STUDY THE WORD

If our prayers are to be effective, it is imperative that we pray according to the will of God. And the Word of God is the best place to find the will of God. The two are actually synonymous. The only way you can know the things that fall into the category of the will of God is by reading and studying the Bible. We need to pray that God will give us a great hunger to study His Word and find out what He has already declared. What changed my prayer life forever is the *Remodel Prayer Card System,* which combines all the Bible prayers that can be prayed for people and condenses them into one easy-to-use system!

Again, it is important to take note of the tense in specific scriptures. When the Word says, "God hath," that means He has already declared or done it. For instance, the Bible tells us that God hath abounded toward us with all wisdom. This means He has already been made wisdom to us. So in the spirit realm, wisdom has already abounded toward us, and Jesus has been made wisdom unto us.

If any of you lacks wisdom, he should ask God, who gives generously to all without finding fault, and it will be given to him. But when he asks, he must believe and not doubt, because he who doubts is like a wave of the sea, blown and tossed by the wind. That man should not think he will receive anything from the Lord; he is a double-minded man, unstable in all he does.

—James 1:5–8

What a comfort to know that God's wisdom is always available to us when we pray with confident and stable faith. When I'm in a jam and don't know what to do, I say, "Lord, I need Your wisdom, and Your Word says that You have been made wisdom unto me. So please show me what I need to know about this situation. I know that wisdom is loosed in heaven, and I'm loosing it in this situation now."

OUR PRAYERS ARE THE PIVOTAL POINTS THAT RELEASE GOD TO MOVE IN THE EARTH.

And He gives it to me. We can also pray wisdom into the lives of other people. You'll learn about how to do this in a later chapter.

Salvation has also been loosed in heaven for all mankind. Jesus purchased it for us on the cross more than 2,000 years ago. The price has already been paid, and everyone can be born again and experience salvation just by asking for forgiveness of their sins and placing their trust in Jesus as the only way to heaven. The Bible tells us that God is *"...not willing that any should perish but that all should come to repentance"* (2 Peter 3:9 NKJV). This means that salvation has already been loosed in heaven, and we can use the key of prayer to loose that salvation on our neighbors, friends, and family.

PRAYERS ARE IMPORTANT PIVOT POINTS

If you are still wondering why you should pray, here it is: As a Christian, you should pray because Jesus has given you the keys to loose and bind what has been loosed and bound in heaven. You have been given an authoritative position on earth, and heaven does not release its goods until you and I begin to pray and loose them into the earth. Our prayers are the pivotal points that release God to move in the earth. Until someone prays, God's hands are tied.

I'm sure there are some religious people who will have "righteous indignation" and say, "What are you talking about? Our God is a sovereign God, and if He wants to do something, He will." I agree that God is sovereign. In fact, He is so sovereign that He will do whatever He said He would do—He won't go back on His Word. And His Word—the Bible—says He has given us the keys and the authority to determine through our prayers what is loosed out of the heavenly realm into the earthly realm.

It is not God's plan that any should perish, and we can pray and ask God to move in the lives of people we know. It is scriptural. We can pray and ask God to change them. If one of your brothers or sisters in Christ gets caught up in carnality, you can pray and ask God to loose a little bit of heaven on them. Instead of falling into the temptation to talk about them, just use your keys and pray for God to release some wisdom and understanding in their lives.

Follow the instructions of Jesus:

> *"This, then, is how you should pray: 'Our Father in heaven, hallowed be your name, your kingdom come, your will be done on earth as it is in heaven.'"*
> —Matthew 6:9,10

In these two verses of what believers have come to call the Lord's Prayer, Jesus provides three specific ways in which we should pray. First, we are to worship Him, speaking of His wonderful, hallowed, and glorious name. Next, we are to pray for His kingdom to come, and then for His will to be done on earth as it is in heaven. Sound familiar? Yes, that's just what I have been sharing with you—loosing what has already been declared in heaven and calling it to the earth.

EVERYTHING THAT GOD IS GOING TO DO FOR YOU, HE HAS ALREADY DONE.

I'm sure you have probably heard a statement that I share with my congregation quite often. *Everything that*

God is going to do for you, He has already done. This statement connects beautifully with the subject of prayer. Someone may say, "But, Pastor, I'm sick and I need God to heal me." Well, I understand that it is the hand of God that touches you, but Jesus has already purchased your healing at Calvary. So you don't have to say, "Oh God, if You can just do it one more time, I need You to heal me." No, that's not necessary. God took care of it once and for all when He allowed His Son to bear stripes upon His back for your healing. Heaven has already declared that healing has been loosed in heaven, and we have the blessed assurance that it is ours when we loose it into our bodies. The question is: how do we bring healing, or whatever God has promised, out of heaven into the earth? Prayer is one of the main vehicles for bringing this to pass.

Jesus said we are to pray that God's kingdom will come, and His kingdom has been described as righteousness, joy, and peace. These are benefits that all of us should enjoy, and we have been given the privilege to pray and loose them into not only our lives but the lives of others. We are also to pray that His will be done here on earth as it is in heaven. We can pray that way because Jesus gave us the keys. He gave us the authority, the right, and the privilege. Who releases the will of God to be done on the earth—you or God? If you and I don't fulfill our responsibility and pray that prayer, we will not see His will done in our lives...or in the lives of others we care about.

Christians determine whether or not God is able to loose and perform His will in the earth. If God could do it—if He had the attitude, "I'll do what I want, so don't worry about it. It's My business, not yours"—why would He tell us in His Word to pray this way? Would Jesus tell us to pray something that would have no effect…something that would be a shot in the dark? No. That's why we know that God doesn't do His will on earth unless somebody prays and asks Him to release to the earth what has already been declared and released in heaven.

AGENTS OF THE ALMIGHTY

It is prayer that moves God to loose what He has already declared and loosed in heaven. The *Remodel Prayer Card System* will categorize all the prayers that the Bible says are God's will for you and me to pray for other people—prayers that will release Him to move in their lives!

WE ARE HIS AGENTS ON EARTH—AGENTS WHO HAVE BEEN PUT HERE TO RELEASE THE THINGS OF GOD INTO PEOPLE'S LIVES.

This is a principle that works every time we pray. If God has declared it, then we have the right to pray and ask God to do it on earth. We are His agents on earth—agents who have been put here to release the things of God into people's lives. You are an agent who can release Him to do His thing!

The Bible says, *The prayer of a righteous man is powerful and effective* (James 5:16). That goes for women too. As agents of God, standing on earth in flesh and blood, our prayers are powerful and cause good things to happen. God has given us keys that enable us to loose heaven's blessing into lives here on earth. What an honor to be an agent of almighty God.

Can you pray a fervent prayer and loose the very blessings of heaven in the earth? You better believe it! That kind of prayer is just what God is waiting for.

Pastor Joe's Main Points Review

1. You can know the will of God before you pray.

2. You can pray with confidence, knowing that God *will* answer your prayers *if* you pray according to His will.

3. When you understand what your prayers can do, then your prayers will have life, and you will have a greater desire to pray.

4. The *Remodel Prayer Card System* will categorize all the prayers that the Bible says are God's will for you to pray for other people, releasing Him to move in their lives.

5. God has given you keys that enable you to loose heaven's blessing into people's lives (including your own) here on earth.

3

What You Pray Matters

E HAVE ALREADY LEARNED THAT JESUS gave us the keys to the kingdom of heaven and that using the keys to the unseen realm can have a powerful impact on our earthly realm. But if we just hang those keys on a hook and choose not to use them to loose or release and to bind or prohibit what's already been done in heaven, we will never reap the benefits of what is available to us. It is not just about releasing good things in our lives, but locking out the things that have been bound.

> PRAYER IS THE NUMBER-ONE VEHICLE THAT CAN BE USED TO RELEASE WHAT HAS BEEN LOOSED IN HEAVEN AND BRING IT IN THE EARTH.

But the things that have been loosed or bound in heaven are not automatically loosed or bound in your life. These things can only be a part of your life when you use the powerful key called prayer. That's why prayer matters. Prayer is the number-one vehicle that can be used to release what has been loosed in heaven and bring it in the earth. That's why prayer is so important.

We have already learned a lot about prayer, but in this chapter, we will learn the importance of *what* we pray in great detail. This is a very important matter, because what we ask for will determine whether or not God gives it to us. This means that it is also important to know the things that are a part of God's will. And we absolutely can know the will of God before we pray.

DON'T NEUTRALIZE YOUR PRAYERS

Christians sometimes pray, "Lord, I have a financial need in my life, and I ask You to meet it, in Jesus' name"—but then they add "if it be Your will." They had a good prayer going until they tacked on the phrase, "if it be Your will." As soon as they said those five little words, their prayer was neutralized and became ineffective. It is sad but true, and many good Christians pray that way simply because they haven't been taught the right way to pray. They assume that adding "if it be Your will," is a good thing that will please God and persuade Him to answer their prayer. But they don't realize that God has given us specific information in the Bible about His general will, and it is our responsibility to dig it out and know it. But if we don't, we will go on praying ineffective, unanswered prayers.

Sometimes people pray, "Lord, my body's sick. I have a problem with my heart. Oh God, heal my heart in Jesus' name, if it be Your will." Again, by adding "if it be Your will," they have gone against the very prayer principles that Jesus taught us, because Jesus taught that we can know His will *before* we pray in certain areas.

As I shared earlier in the book, sometimes it is appropriate to add, "if it be Your will." A good example is Jesus' prayer in the Garden of Gethsemane. It was almost time for Him to face going to the cross, and He was agonizing in prayer over the pain and suffering that was involved in dying on a cross. It was common knowledge that it involved brutal torture and excruciating pain, and Jesus, in a flesh-and-blood body, was keenly aware of what was before Him. And He cried out,

> "...O My Father, if it is possible, let this cup pass
> from Me; nevertheless, not as I will, but as You will."
> —Matthew 26:39 NKJV

This is how it should be for all of us. When it comes to what we do with our lives, we must have that same attitude—"not my will but Your will be done." Sometimes when I'm presented with opportunities, at first I'm not sure what the will of God is, so I begin to pray, "Lord, not my will but Your will be done." And many times when God reveals His will to me, it hurts my flesh to do it—it's painful. So it was with Jesus. Accomplishing God's will on the cross literally hurt His flesh, and He agonized over it, but in the end He chose God's will. And in some situations, we too must choose God's will over our own.

PREPARE YOURSELF TO PRAY WITH CONFIDENCE

I believe the Bible has already shown us what the will of God is for certain things.

> *This is the confidence we* [Christians] *have in approaching God: that if we ask anything according to his will, he hears us. And if we know that he hears us—whatever we ask—we know that we have what we asked of him.*
>
> —1 John 5:14,15

These verses contain three powerful and positive phrases that are easily understood.

1. *This is the confidence we have in approaching God.* Before we approach God, we should have confidence that He's going to hear us. And the only way we can have confidence when we pray is to know God's will concerning the thing we're asking of Him.

2. *If we ask anything according to His will, He hears us.*
Now, if we stopped here we would be in trouble
because we could say, "if it be
Your will" at the end of every
prayer. But God's Word clearly
specifies many things that
are His will, and we have the
responsibility of searching out
the information provided there. God will show us His
will when it is not clear to us, but we must be diligent
to read the Word and pray according to His stated will.
If we don't have confidence when we pray, it is because
we don't know God's will concerning the thing we're
asking of Him.

> WE MUST BE DILIGENT TO READ THE WORD AND PRAY ACCORDING TO HIS STATED WILL.

3. *We know that we have what we asked of him.* In other
words, as soon as we finish praying, we should know
that we have what we asked of God. But we can only
have that assurance when we know that we have
approached Him in confidence and prayed according
to His will.

If there are scriptures declaring God's will about the
thing we are praying for, we must have those scriptures
in our hearts and pray accordingly. But for situations in
which there are no biblical statements regarding His
specific will—perhaps, whether to take this job or that job

or which church you should attend—it is appropriate to pray, "Lord, show me Your will concerning the job You want me to have (or the church You want me to attend)." But for many of the needs in our lives, we can and must know the will of God before we pray. Only then can we know that we have what we asked of Him.

How can you know you received it if you're not sure God wants you to have it? And you can't know that He wants you to have it unless you know that it is His will. Therefore, in order to know that it is His will and that He wants you to have it, you must know ahead of time that it belongs to you.

STAY CONNECTED TO THE VINE

Jesus said the same thing in a different way in John 15 where He tells us that He is the vine and we are the branches, and stresses the importance of staying connected to Him:

> *"If you stay joined to me and my words remain in you, you may ask any request you like, and it will be granted."*
>
> —John 15:7 NLT

Now, that is very clear, and it sounds pretty positive. When we stay connected to the Vine—when we are born again and in fellowship with Him—God will give us what we request of Him. But if we're out of fellowship with God—disconnected in our hearts—then we don't have confidence, and we can't release faith.

If we remain in fellowship with Him and His Word is in us, He will grant us whatever we ask. The will of God is revealed in His Word, and if you have the Word in you and you make a request according to that Word, He will give you what He said belongs to you.

Here's the key. If you really want to enhance your prayer life, you must study the Word of God and know what the Bible says. The Word reveals what has been loosed and bound in heaven, and when you know that, you can pray those things in the earth. Ephesians 1:3 tells us that God *...has blessed us with every spiritual blessing in the heavenly places in Christ* (NKJV). We can pull those blessings out of that heavenly realm into our earthly realm and have them operating in our lives.

JOY DOES NOT DEPEND ON YOUR CIRCUMSTANCES.

Did you know that joy does not depend on your circumstances? Joy is a spiritual blessing that has been released in heaven, and you can walk in joy every day of your life. You can have an internal party going on no matter what kind of storm you're walking in, because joy is a blessing that God said belongs to you.

Peace is a spiritual blessing that heaven has released, and you can pull it into your life. And there is nothing on this planet that is more awesome than the peace of God. When your soul is in turmoil, it weakens your immune system and opens you up to every kind of physical problem and disease, because stress is the number-one thing that opens you up to physical destruction. But peace does

THE PEACE OF GOD IS THERE JUST WAITING FOR US.

not depend on your circumstances or who you are. Peace is a spiritual blessing that has been released in heaven, and you have a right to have it operating in your life.

We don't have to wait for God to give us peace. We can take all we want because it belongs to us. And if we are oppressed, it is simply because we haven't given our cares to the Lord, and released some of His peace into our lives—because the peace of God is there just waiting for us.

Everything that God could ever do for you, He has already done. And His will is revealed. Jesus tells us to pray the Lord's Prayer—"*thy will be done in earth, as it is in heaven*" (KJV). It's a done deal, and all we have to do is pray it into the earth. If heaven has loosed it, we have a right to bring it into our lives.

GOD WANTS TO MEET YOUR NEEDS

Philippians 4 talks about the fact that God wants to meet our needs. In the preceding verses, Paul tells the Philippian church how much he appreciates their faithfulness in giving to help him do the work of the ministry. He thanks them for being a blessing to him, and then he says,

> *This same God who takes care of me will supply all your needs from his glorious riches, which have been given to us in Christ Jesus.*
>
> —Philippians 4:19 NLT

There are many verses in the Bible that assure us that it is God's will to meet our needs, but there are other scriptures that we must consider—like 2 Thessalonians 3:10, which says if we don't work we shouldn't eat, and Proverbs 13:4, which says if we are sluggards God won't bless us, but if we're diligent, God will bless us. So we have some responsibility in the matter.

If we are working hard and doing everything we know to do, and we're just not making enough to take care of our needs, the will of God is to bless us. According to Phillipians 4:19, He wants to supply all of our needs according to His riches in glory. And there is no shortage of riches in heaven!

Another thing to consider is the revelation of tithing found in the Bible. I've been tithing since I was a very young Christian. The first time I read about tithing in the Bible, it shocked me. I nearly had a heart attack because I found out that the tithe meant giving a tenth of my income to the Lord, and I almost passed out. But then I prayed and asked God to help me. And once I saw it, God held me responsible to do it. If you don't know and understand it, God will supply your needs whether you do it or not. But once you understand what the tithe is all about, you are accountable to God. The tithe is all about supplying the needs of the church, the preacher, and other church employees. And if you are not tithing, their needs are not being met.

So it would be hard to say, "Lord, meet my need," when you're not being obedient to tithe and meet the needs of the church you attend. But if you're walking in the light that you have, you have every right to go to God and say, "I have a need, and I'm asking You to meet it." And when you do, God will meet the need according to His riches in glory.

IS IT THE WILL OF GOD TO HEAL YOUR BODY? YOU BETTER BELIEVE IT IS.

Another thing that we can be sure of is that God wants to heal us. First Peter 2:24 tells us that by the stripes of Jesus we *were* healed. So if I am healed, I don't have to keep asking God to heal me, because I am already healed. And Psalm 103:3 says, *He forgives all my sins and heals all my diseases* (NLT).

> *Is any one of you sick? He should call the elders of the church to pray over him and anoint him with oil in the name of the Lord. And the prayer offered in faith will make the sick person well; the Lord will raise him up....*
>
> —James 5:14,15

Is it the will of God to heal your body? You better believe it is. And once you know that, do you have a right to go to God and say, "Father, I have a problem in my body, and I ask You in the name of Jesus to heal it"? Do you have the right to believe that He heard you and has healed you? Absolutely, because you know that it is the will of God. Healing has been loosed in heaven, and God will give it to you when you ask for it.

Does God want to get inside people and change them and make them Christlike? He does. As I pointed out in a previous chapter:

> *For God is working in you* [Christians], *giving you the desire to obey him and the power to do what pleases him.*
> —Philippians 2:13 NLT

And the first chapter of Philippians says:

> *I am sure that God, who began the good work within you, will continue his work until it is finally finished on that day when Christ Jesus comes back again.*
> —Philippians 1:6 NLT

The reason we pray and ask God to move in people's lives is because He has let us know that it is His will to do so.

HEALED AND CHANGED BY
THE POWER OF GOD

I recently experienced the most awesome blessing from heaven. I was close to a man who fell into terrible chemical and alcohol dependency. It broke my heart, and I was trying to help him, but he didn't want help. I said, "I think you need professional help. Allow me to hook you up with a good Christian professional to help you." And he got so mad at me that he told me off and ended our relationship. But I kept praying and asking God to rescue him from his dependencies, using the detailed prayers under the "R" in the *Remodel Prayer Card System.*

I knew that he was dealing with severe insecurities and fear caused from growing up in a terrible home environment, and I loved him and wanted to see God heal him and change his life.

A couple of years later, I was walking out of a restaurant, and this man walked up to me and said, "I want to apologize for everything I've said and done. I've got my life together now, and I'm free from the dependencies." It was a wonderful, touching reunion, and I was so happy that I wanted to cry.

A short while later, he told me that he had been free from his chemical and alcohol dependencies for a year. It was obvious that his life had been changed. It was hard to believe that he was the same person I had known before— it was like talking to a different person. He shared how bad the dependency had been, and related an incident in which he was driving in a vehicle with his boss. As they passed one of our church billboards with my picture on it, he said he made an obscene gesture and told me off. His boss said, "You have to get that right." And he said, "I'll never get it right." But he went on to tell how God did a

PRAYER WILL WORK FOR ANY KIND OF NEED WHEN WE PRAY TO THE FATHER IN JESUS' NAME.

miraculous work in his life. And he said, "Now, every time I pass an empty billboard, I pray, 'Lord God, give that to Pastor Joe at Believers' Christian Fellowship, and let them spread the gospel in the greatest way they can." This man is now living for God, and our relationship is restored! I believe my prayers and the prayers of others released God to move and change him from the inside out!

God changes people, and you probably have some loved ones that God wants to change. My word to you is: don't give up on them. If heaven has loosed what they need, you have a right to pray it into their lives. Prayer will work for any kind of need—salvation, healing, marriage, finances, whatever—when we pray to the Father in Jesus' name.

The Bible says if we know the will of God and pray the will of God, then we know that God hears us and will answer our prayers. So if you know that what you are praying for has been released in heaven, you know that it is yours, and you can believe that you receive it and thank Him for it before you get it.

Pastor Joe's Main Points Review

1. Prayer is the number-one vehicle that you can use to release what has been loosed in heaven and bring it into the earth.

2. When it comes to what you do with your life, your attitude needs to be, "not my will but Your will be done, Lord."

3. The general will of God has already been determined, and your prayers can release it into the earth!

4. God changes people—even your loved ones—so don't give up on them. Your prayers will work for any kind of need when you pray the will of God as found in the Bible.

4

Who You Pray to Matters

WE KNOW THAT PRAYER MATTERS AND THAT it is an important part of a Christian's life. But equally important is who we pray to.

This is an important principle that most of us know. In fact, if I were to ask a group of people who had been Christians for any length of time, "Who do you pray to?" most of them would say, "I pray to God the Father in the name of Jesus." This is the correct answer, and when we truly understand all the wonderful privileges we have been given it is cause for great rejoicing. We have the right to pray to the Father in Jesus' name, and to use the keys to the kingdom of heaven.

It is a great honor to have been given the keys that open up a more effective prayer life, because no one likes to pray and not receive answers. And praying to the Father in Jesus' name is one principle we must use if we want our prayers to be answered.

In John 16:23, Jesus makes this interesting statement, *"In that day you will ask Me nothing..."* (NKJV). "That day" refers to the day we are living in right now. In verses 16 through 22, Jesus talked to the disciples about His death, burial, and Resurrection. And, understandably, they were sad about it.

But then He mentioned "that day," referring to the time after He is raised from the dead. Actually, further study of the Bible reveals that "that day" encompasses the time from Jesus' Resurrection to the time when He returns to earth to take us home to heaven, the Second Coming of Christ. The twelve disciples heard about "that day" directly from the lips of Jesus, but those words also apply to us, His disciples today, and to every disciple who will ever live on the earth.

JESUS TELLS US HOW TO PRAY AND GET ANSWERS.

So Jesus is saying to all of His disciples, "During the time you're living on earth, this is how you should pray." Then He lays out the instructions for us: "In that day, you will ask me [Jesus] nothing." He is saying to us, "Don't pray to Me. Don't ask Me for anything." Then He goes on to say,

"...Most assuredly, I say to you, whatever you ask the Father in My name He will give you. Until now you have asked nothing in My name. Ask, and you will receive, that your joy may be full."

—John 16:23,24 NKJV

Wow! Jesus tells us how to pray and get answers, and in the deal, He assures us that we will receive fullness of joy. Now, that's something to get excited about!

ADDRESS THE FATHER IN JESUS' NAME

That scripture alone is awesome, but in Matthew 6, Jesus gives us further instruction about how to pray.

"This, then, is how you should pray: 'Our Father in heaven, hallowed be your name, your kingdom come, your will be done on earth as it is in heaven.'"

—Matthew 6:9,10

This scripture tells us to pray to God the Father—not Jesus, but God the Father. Jesus is saying, "When you pray, address God the Father." It is so simple and elementary, but so very important. Then He says we should pray that the Father's kingdom would come and that His will would be done on earth. In these two Scripture passages, we can clearly see that we are to address God the Father.

Now, the apostle Paul was one of the greatest apostles who ever walked on the earth, and Jesus called him to literally finish writing the Bible. He wrote nearly three quarters of the New Testament. He was a great man of God who had the greatest call in the church that has ever existed. He was also a great man of prayer, and he prayed according to the instructions of Jesus.

> *For this reason I bow my knees to the Father of our Lord Jesus Christ, from whom the whole family in heaven and earth is named, that He* [God the Father] *would grant you, according to the riches of His glory, to be strengthened with might through His Spirit in the inner man.*
>
> —Ephesians 3:14–16 NKJV

Jesus is God the Son, but Paul is praying to His Father, God the Father.

In addition to addressing God the Father, Paul used the keys that we talked about earlier. One of the things he prayed was that God the Father would release the Holy Spirit into the lives of Christians to strengthen them from the inside. Now, that's an exciting prayer that you and I can pray also. I'll address praying this way when we examine the second "E" in our *Remodel Prayer Card System* in chapter twelve.

WE MUST PRAY TO GOD THE FATHER IN JESUS' NAME.

In heaven, the Holy Spirit is as loosed as He can be. God has given us all the Holy Spirit that He will ever give us. So we have the right to take the Holy Spirit that is in the unseen realm of heaven and pray Him into our earthly realm. And one of the ways we can do that is to pray and ask God to fill people with the Holy Spirit and release His supernatural strength on the inside of them. If you know people who are weary and ready to throw in the towel, you can pray and ask God to release the Holy Spirit in their lives. You can pray and literally loose the Holy Spirit to strengthen them and give them the ability to live for God. You and I have that right because God has given us the keys to the kingdom of heaven. But remember that we must pray to God the Father *in Jesus' name.*

Why did Jesus tell us to ask in His name? When we accepted Jesus as our Savior, God made us righteous, holy, and blameless, and we now have the right to go to the throne of God with our requests. Isn't it exciting to know that we can talk to the Father? Going through an earthly mediator is not necessary anymore. In the Old Covenant, people had to go through the priests, but we don't have to do that—we can go directly to God because we have been made righteous in the sight of God because of what Jesus did for us at Calvary.

When Jesus told the twelve disciples to pray to the Father in Jesus' name, they didn't have trouble understanding it. They instantly knew what He meant. And when we understand what they understood, we too will instantly know what Jesus meant. The phrase "in my name" is a legal term, or we could say it is a kingdom term. And it is interesting to learn how kingdoms and the legal system worked in Bible days.

THE RIGHT-HAND MAN

Oftentimes, a king would appoint a person—someone he really trusted and believed in—and give him all authority in his kingdom. This person had full authority, and when he spoke, it was the same as if the king had spoken. This powerful man had authority to do whatever he wanted to do, whenever and wherever he wanted to do it. His position—seated at the right hand of the king—signified his power and authority. And when the king had to be away, perhaps leading a campaign or waging war, this high-level official was in charge, and everyone understood that.

If this official needed something from the king while he was away, he would prepare a document, put his seal on it, and send somebody to deliver it to the king. That seal was the same as his name, and when the king saw it, he knew immediately who it was from and that it represented official business. And because the messenger brought a request in the name of the man who was in charge of the kingdom, he could approach the king and instantly receive whatever was requested, whether it was gold, food, or some other necessary commodity. As far as the king was concerned, it was the same as if his official had walked in and asked for it.

That's how it worked in Bible days. So when Jesus told the disciples they were to pray to the Father in His name, they instantly understood what He was saying. It is a good example for Christians today of how important it is to do the same. Look at a couple of scriptures that will help you understand it better and tie it all together. The apostle Peter tells us that Jesus *has gone into heaven and is at God's right hand—with angels, authorities and powers in submission to him* (1 Peter 3:22). Most Christians know that Jesus is seated at the right hand of Father God, and that He has authority over everything in the kingdom of heaven. It is a situation similar to the earthly king appointing a man to have authority over his earthly kingdom, although the spiritual impact of Jesus' power is significantly more important.

> *God exalted him* [Jesus] *to the highest place and gave him the name that is above every name, that at the name of Jesus every knee should bow, in heaven and on earth and under the earth, and every tongue confess that Jesus Christ is Lord, to the glory of God the Father.*
>
> —Philippians 2:9–11

EXTREME Prayer MAKEOVER

God sat Jesus right there at His right hand—the highest place of honor He could have had. And everybody and everything bows at the mention of the name of Jesus—even in heaven.

WE HAVE THE KEYS TO THAT HEAVENLY REALM WHERE JESUS IS SEATED AT THE RIGHT HAND OF GOD THE FATHER.

Ephesians records the words of Paul as he prayed that the saints might know God's great power and the mighty strength...

Which he exerted in Christ when he raised him from the dead and seated him at his right hand in the heavenly realms, far above all rule and authority, power and dominion, and every title that can be given, not only in the present age but also in the one to come.

—Ephesians 1:20,21

Think about that. We have the keys to that heavenly realm where Jesus is seated at the right hand of God the Father. Understanding the truth of this revelation should bring great excitement to the very core of our being!

Jesus wants us to know that when we pray, we have every right to address God one on one and express our needs—not because of our goodness but because we are righteous and holy through Christ. Jesus made it simple for us by giving us authority. He said, "Here is My seal, which gives you the authority to pray to God the Father *in My name*, asking for whatever you need, and He will give it to you." Why does He give us what we need? Because as far as God is concerned, when we pray to Him in the name of Jesus, it is the same as if Jesus himself were standing before God asking for something.

That is exciting, and when you take hold of that it will make a difference in your prayer life. When you really understand that who you pray to matters, you will experience confidence that you've never had before. When you know that praying to the Father in Jesus' name brings results, you will want to spend more time in prayer.

I consider myself to be a mature Christian, and I go after God with everything I've got, but sometimes at the end of the day, I feel that I didn't do enough. I can think of things that I shouldn't have said or done. But it's so wonderful to know that I am the righteousness of God in Christ Jesus, and I'm holy and blameless—and you are too if you are a Christian who is doing your best to live for God. It gives us blessed peace and confidence to know that when we pray to the Father in Jesus' name, He will answer our prayers. It is exciting to know that when I say "in Jesus' name," it's not just a common phrase

WHEN YOU USE THE NAME OF JESUS, IT IS THE SAME AS IF JESUS SAID IT.

or a cliché. I'm saying to God the Father, "Here's the seal." And God the Father is saying, "Well, I'm giving this to you because you asked in Jesus' name—not because of who and what you are but because of who He is.

We can also use that name in other ways on this earth. The Bible tells us that *everything* is subject to that name. So the next time you sense a feeling of oppression or fear, say, "Devil, I rebuke this fear that you're trying to put on me, and I command you to go in the name of Jesus." When you use the name of Jesus, it is the same as if Jesus said it, and everything has to bow to His name. It won't happen because you flex your natural or spiritual muscles or scream and shout, but it will happen because you used the name that's above every other name.

Prayer works here on earth when we use the keys to the kingdom and take authority over everyday situations. Jesus gave us the keys to use, and He said, "Hey, saints, whatever is loosed up here in the heavenly realm can be loosed on earth by praying to the Father in My name. It's a legal matter, a kingdom matter, and I have given you authority."

If Jesus said it, it is true. So pray to the one who really matters in the name of Jesus, and get ready for an influx of answers.

Pastor Joe's Main Points Review

1. God's Word gives specific instructions on how to pray and get answers.

2. Your prayers must be addressed to God the Father, not to Jesus.

3. You can pray and ask God to release the Holy Spirit in the lives of people you know who are weary and ready to give up, and the Holy Spirit will strengthen them and give them the ability to live for God.

4. When you use the name of Jesus, it is the same as if Jesus said it, and *everything* has to bow to His name.

5

How You Pray Matters

WONDER HOW MANY PEOPLE REALLY GIVE serious thought to *how* they pray. I believe that a lot of folks just pray whatever is on their mind, without realizing that *how* they pray has a very definite impact on whether or not their prayers are answered. There is a little phrase that's used throughout the Bible, and if you really want answers to your prayers—and why wouldn't you?—it's necessary to understand its importance. Throughout the Bible, we are encouraged to pray and ask God for whatever we need—and we usually see the words "in faith." In this chapter, we're going to take a closer look at what the Bible says about praying in faith.

James 1:1–4 talks about the tribulations, trials, and the tough times that we have to deal with from time to time in our lives. That is a given—as long as we walk on this earth, we're going to have challenges and difficult times in our lives. And sometimes when we're going through a tough time, we're not sure what to do. We're not sure what the next step should be, and we wonder, *What should I do to get out of this?* James provides the answer:

> *If any of you lacks wisdom, let him ask of God, who gives to all liberally and without reproach, and it will be given to him.*
>
> —James 1:5 NKJV

RECEIVE WISDOM WITHOUT REPROACH

This verse lets us know that it is the will of God to give us wisdom. If you lack wisdom, and you are uncertain about what steps to take in a particular situation, God wants to give it to you. This prayer also works when we're not in trouble but simply want God to flood us with His will or wisdom regarding a decision we need to make in a particular area. He tells us in this verse what to do. We are to ask God, who will then give to us generously and without reproach. *Reproach* means, "blame; rebuke." I find it both comforting and exciting to know that when I say, "Father, I'm in a jam, and I need some help," God isn't going to blame me or rebuke me, saying, "If you hadn't done such and such, you wouldn't be in this jam." No. He loves us and wants to help us.

Now, in the often-trying task of teaching our kids to do right things and to do things right, they sometimes make mistakes. When they do, as parents we sometimes have a tendency to make sure they understand that it was what they did wrong that

> WE ARE HIS CHILDREN, AND HE LOVES US AND WANTS TO GIVE US WISDOM.

got them into the jam in the first place. And while it is true that they must learn from their mistakes, we can lovingly help them see their error and then quickly give them the benefit of our wisdom without condemning them. This is the way God does it.

It has been my experience that when I go to God and say, "Father, I don't know how to get out of this mess, and I need Your wisdom," He doesn't blame or rebuke me. He doesn't say, "Well, you deserve it. Don't you realize what you did? Just suffer for a little while." No, He gives me wisdom without blaming or rebuking me. And He does that for all of us. We are His children, and He loves us and wants to give us wisdom so we can get out of trouble. That's the kind of God we serve.

Sometimes I'm in trouble through no fault of my own. But at other times I make bad decisions—wrong choices that end up getting me in a jam...just like you do. But when I get in a jam because of wrong choices, God wants to get me out of it just as much as He does when it isn't my fault. And He wants to get you out of your jams too. Now, I'm sure that He wants us to learn from our mistakes, but the very fact that we realize our position and recognize our need of His wisdom is a positive step in the right direction.

It goes without saying that all of us are a mess compared to Jesus, the standard. God already knows that we get into messes in our lives and that without His help we can't always get out of them. But when we recognize our need and say, "Lord, I want to get out of this, and I'm asking You to give me wisdom," He will do it. The Bible says it is His will to give us wisdom.

> CAN YOU REALLY SAY THAT YOU PRAY IN FAITH...WITH NO DOUBTING?

ASK IN FAITH—WITH NO DOUBTING

In James, he gives further instruction about *how* we are to ask:

> *But let him ask in faith, with no doubting, for he who doubts is like a wave of the sea driven and tossed by the wind. For let not that man suppose that he will receive anything from the Lord; he is a double-minded man, unstable in all his ways.*
>
> —James 1:6–8 NKJV

Now, if you just quickly read that verse, you may think, "Yes, I know that's right." But when you put yourself in the picture, can you really say that you pray *in faith…with no doubting?* It's easy to read, but it's a bit more difficult to do. That's why it is so important to make sure that we really believe, without a doubt, that God will give us what we ask for in prayer.

Faith is the opposite of doubt, and if we have the slightest reservation about whether or not God will hear and answer our prayers, we are harboring doubt. And the Bible says if we doubt when we pray, there is no need for us to think that we will receive from God. So when we pray and are convinced that what we have requested is as good as done, we have prayed

FAITH IS A RESULT OF KNOWING WHAT GOD PROMISED US!

in faith. But if, after we pray, we don't feel the assurance that the answer is on the way, then we have not prayed in total faith. We are harboring some doubt.

So how can we pray and not doubt? We have to know the will of God before we pray. And when we pray the will of God, which is found in His Word, we can pray with confidence, knowing, without a doubt, that He heard us and the answer is on the way. We dealt with this revelation in chapter 3, and it's important to note that faith is a result of knowing what God promised us!

John G. Lake was a great man of God who lived in our century. He was one of the greatest preachers who ever walked on this earth, and he said something in one of his sermons that I think is just absolutely outstanding. He said, "Beloved, it is not our long prayers but our believing God that gets the answer."[1]

Too many people believe that they must pray long prayers with just the proper words and phrases, but God cares much more about the condition of our hearts and our ability to be open, honest, and believing.

DANCING WITH A DEMON

I remember the first time I tried to cast out a demon—it was in 1984. Now, I'm not a demon hunter, but when the need arises, I am obedient to the will of God. One day Gina and I were working at the church, which was only a year old at the time, when some men of our church brought a man in off the street and said, "He needs prayer." As I began to pray for him, the Spirit of God spoke to me that he had a devil in him. I was shocked, but I knew that a devil was no match for the Master. So I said, "Devil, I command you to come out in the name of Jesus." And immediately the hair on the back of my head stood up. The man's voice changed, and in a deep, awkward voice, he said, "I didn't come in here for this. I came in

[1] www.holybible.com/resources/poems/ps.php?sid=261

for prayer." Now, I had read about demon possession and casting them out of people, and I had even taught on it, but this was my first "up close and personal" confrontation with one, and I was like "Whoa." It about scared me out of my wits. But I knew that it was God's will for people to be delivered from demons, and I was willing for Him to work through me to deliver this man. I spent about four hours dancing with this demon—"Come out!" "No, I'm not going to come out"...and on and on it went, for close to four hours.

A friend of ours, George Moss, was preaching for us that week, and he was staying at our house. And about that time, he suddenly knew that he needed to come to the church. So I'm in there still dancing with this demon, and in walks George with a smile on his face. And when he came in, the demon-possessed man stopped and looked at him, and then he started mocking and laughing at George. As George moved closer, the man shut up. But here's what bugged me. For almost four hours, I had been saying the perfect thing: "Come out in the name of Jesus," and then George walks in and says, "Loose him!" And that's all it took. The guy collapsed. He fell on the floor, got up, and got saved and filled with the Holy Ghost in just a couple of minutes.

Now, I was embarrassed, but I learned something that I've never forgotten. If we believe that what we say is going to happen, there is power behind our words. And if we pray and believe that God heard us, there is power behind those words that causes heaven to move. George *believed* that his words would work, and I *hoped* that mine would work! You now know which one worked and which one didn't! You and I have to be convinced what the will of God is before we pray, and then we can pray with confidence. How we pray matters!

When Jesus walked on the earth, there were times when even the Son of God couldn't perform miracles. There were times when He couldn't bring things out of heaven into earth like He wanted to. Consider this passage of Scripture:

> When Jesus had finished these parables, he moved on from there. Coming to his hometown, he began teaching the people in their synagogue, and they were amazed. "Where did this man get this wisdom and these miraculous powers?" they asked. "Isn't this the carpenter's son? Isn't his mother's name Mary, and aren't his brothers James, Joseph, Simon and Judas? Aren't all his sisters with us? Where then did this man get all these things?" And they took offense at him. But Jesus said to them, "Only in his hometown and in his own house is a prophet without honor." And he did not do many miracles there because of their lack of faith.
>
> —Matthew 13:53–58

Mark 6 says it this way:

> *He could not do any miracles there, except lay his*
> *hands on a few sick people and heal them. And he was*
> *amazed at their lack of faith.*
>
> —Mark 6:5,6

People's lack of faith in Jesus' ability stopped Jesus, the Son of God, from bringing miracles out of heaven into the earth. And if a lack of faith could stop Jesus from performing miracles on the earth, do you think a lack of faith can stop our prayers from being answered? Absolutely. If Jesus couldn't do the things He wanted to do because of people's lack of faith, then when we have a lack of faith and don't pray in faith, our prayers are hindered. But if we pray in faith and believe that what we asked for is given to us, we can release those things out of heaven into the earth.

Mark 5:22–34, presents the story about a man and a woman—both with great needs—who had great faith. The man was Jairus, and he came to Jesus and said, "My daughter is dying. Would you come and heal her?" And Jesus said yes, and He began to follow Jairus. The Bible tells us that as they were walking, there was a large crowd just thronging Jesus. And everybody was touching Him, which wasn't unusual in that day. People wanted to touch the man of God.

In the crowd of people around Jesus was a woman who had an internal bleeding problem. She had gone to the best doctors of that day and spent all the money she had, but the Bible says she only grew worse. Nobody could help her. So when she heard about Jesus, the man who called himself the Son of God, and learned that He had been healing people and raising the dead, she knew that she had to get to Him. She was told that at the touch of Jesus, blind people could see, deaf people could hear, cripples could walk, and lepers were cleansed. And the Bible tells us that when she heard this, she said, *"If only I may touch His clothes, I shall be made well"* (v. 28, NKJV).

Now is that a faith statement? Is there any doubt in that statement? "If only I may touch His clothes, I shall be made well." It is perfectly clear that when she said that, she believed it in her heart—so much so that she was willing to push her way through the throng of people to get to Jesus. And her tenacity paid off—finally she saw Jesus, and reached out and touched His clothes. The Bible tells us that immediately power went out of Him and healed her.

Then Jesus said, "Who touched me?" And the disciples said, "Master, hundreds of people are touching You, so why do You ask, "Who touched Me?" And Jesus said, "No, somebody touched Me" (paraphrased). And the woman came and knelt down in front of Him and told Him everything that had happened—how she had been dying because no one could stop the bleeding inside…and how she had heard that He was healing all kinds of sickness. Then she told Him that she knew if she could just touch His clothes, she would be healed. And Jesus said, *"Daughter, your faith has made you well…"* (v. 34 NKJV).

DON'T LET THE STRIKES IN YOUR PRAYER LIFE DISCOURAGE YOU.

Now, hundreds of people touched Jesus that day and did not experience His healing power. But when this woman touched Him, the power came out of Him and went into her. And Jesus basically said, "Your faith pulled that power out of Me."

RELEASE THE POWER OF HEAVEN

Some of us have prayed and believed, but we didn't get an answer. If that has happened to you, I encourage you not to give up. In baseball, if your batting average is 300, that means you hit three out of ten balls, which means you strike out or get thrown out seven out of ten times. Yet if you have a 300 batting average in baseball, you're an incredible hitter. So don't let the strikes in your prayer life discourage you.

I believe God wants us to bat 100 percent in our faith. But if you're only batting one out of ten times with your faith, just keep going after it. Keep growing. Don't stop believing God, because the Bible is true. And if you can believe it, your faith can pull it in. So don't get lost thinking about what you did wrong or why it didn't work. Just keep doing what the Word of God says, and the percentage of answered prayers will just continue to go higher and higher. Be like the woman who touched Jesus' clothes—reach out with your faith and pull in the thing you need.

Hundreds and thousands of people pray, crying out to God to do this or that, and nothing happens. But when people pray in faith

AS WE LEARN TO PRAY IN FAITH, WE HAVE MUCH GREATER SUCCESS WITH OUR PRAYERS.

and believe that they received what they asked for, the things that have been loosed in heaven are released to come into the earth. I like to say it this way: faith is the currency of heaven. Faith is like a hand, and when we pray, it pulls things out of the unseen realm and brings them into this earthly realm. And as we learn to pray in faith, we have much greater success with our prayers.

> *"Therefore I say to you, whatever things you ask when you pray, believe that you receive them, and you will have them."*
>
> —Mark 11:24 NKJV

Notice that the answers to our prayers don't show up in our lives until we believe we receive them when we ask. Praying in faith is simply believing that God gave it to you when you asked for it. I believe that God is giving you revelation in this book that will take you further in your prayer life than you have ever been before. Knowing how to pray makes a difference, so I encourage you to keep believing that you are receiving the things you ask of God.

I love the safety of praying the Word of God. We're not trying to make God do what we want, but we're discovering what He has promised us and what He has already done for us.

Pastor Joe's Main Points Review

1. God will give you wisdom when you are uncertain about what steps to take in a particular situation.

2. When you pray in faith, (and don't doubt), and believe that what you asked for is given to you, you can release those things out of heaven into the earth.

3. Keep doing what the Word of God says, and your answered prayers will continue to increase.

4. Praying in faith is simply believing that God gave it to you when you asked for it.

6

What You Do after You Pray Matters

E HAVE ALREADY LEARNED THE importance of knowing how we should pray, but I wonder how many people really know and understand what they should do *after* they pray. We can pray and ask God to meet our needs, believe that we receive it, and even give thanks for it. But what happens when we wake up the next day and nothing has changed? Or three days or a week later, and nothing's changed? What do we do then? This chapter will give you some insight, but the first thing you must know is that what you do *after* you pray *really* matters.

We often cancel out our prayers by doing the wrong thing after we pray—like getting out of faith and letting go of what we believed we had received. So often we lose what we prayed for, and then we think, *Well, should I pray again, or what should I do?* When these kinds of thoughts begin to bombard our minds, we must understand that what we do after we pray really matters. We must be determined to hold on and keep believing until something happens.

KEEP BELIEVING UNTIL SOMETHING HAPPENS.

THE PEOPLE FACTOR

There are two main factors that hinder our prayers from being answered right away. One is the *people factor*. When God answers our prayers, He often has to use a person. Sometimes we're that person, and sometimes it's somebody else. But many times we pray, and in order for God to give us what we asked for, it has to come through the hands of another person. And when that is the case, we have the people factor. And when God's dealing with people, it can take some time.

I can tell you that in my own life, there are two things I deal with when God instructs me to write a check or do something to bless someone else. This person has prayed for something, and God wants to use me to be that blessing. But too often when God speaks to me, I begin to wonder if it is really God telling me to do it. Sometimes I know it is God, but if He is asking me to do something that is a little bigger than I'm ready to do, I sometimes dig my heels in and argue with Him. I don't do it in a mean way. I just say, "Are You sure, Lord, that if I write that check, I'll be okay?" And God has to keep dealing with me to get me to do it.

GOD OFTEN ANSWERS OUR PRAYERS THROUGH PEOPLE.

But I can tell you from experience that every time I have obeyed God when He has dealt with me to write a check or do something else to bless someone, I've always received a harvest quickly. Yet I seem to struggle when God deals with me about doing something that's bigger than I think I'm able to do at that particular moment. So God often answers our prayers through people. And we must understand that sometimes it just takes a while for people to get in agreement with God. And it helps if we can remember that so we don't make the same mistake.

When I was a young Christian, I would pray for something, and then I'd begin to wonder who was capable of answering that prayer. I almost got mad at people when they didn't respond. But God can bring things to you through people that you never expected He would use. And don't start trying to figure out who it's going to come from. Don't think, *I don't know anyone God could use to answer this prayer.* You don't need to worry about it. It may take a little longer because of the people factor, but you can be sure that when God moves through people, He will get that thing to you.

THE ENEMY FACTOR

The other factor that we have to be aware of is the *enemy factor*. Our enemy also lives in the unseen realm, and he does everything within his power to stop good things from manifesting in our lives, including taking advantage of the *people factor*. God will deal with people about doing a particular thing for someone, and the enemy will quickly bring thoughts to their minds that maybe it wasn't really God and they probably shouldn't do it.

At other times, people aren't needed at all for you to receive God's answer to your prayer. The Bible is very clear about many things that are God's will for us, and we have every right to pray and expect to receive those things. But there are powers, even in the unseen realm that will try to hold us back from praying for and receiving those things.

An excellent example of this is found in Daniel 10:12–14. I believe that God made sure this passage of Scripture was recorded so we would be able to understand what happens behind the scenes. Daniel had sought the Lord, inquiring of Him concerning Israel and their future, and weeks and weeks had passed without an answer. Finally an angel showed up and said something that is very revealing:

"Do not be afraid, Daniel. Since the first day that you set your mind to gain understanding and to humble yourself before your God, your words were heard, and I have come in response to them. But the prince of the Persian kingdom resisted me twenty-one days. Then Michael, one of the chief princes, came to help me, because I was detained there with the king of Persia. Now I have come to explain to you what will happen to your people in the future, for the vision concerns a time yet to come."

—Daniel 10:12–14

God answered Daniel's prayer the second he prayed, and dispatched an angel to go to him. But the angel was delayed when the prince of Persia stopped him and wouldn't allow him to get through.

Now, the prince of Persia was not a person—it was a demonic host that was over the nation of Persia, and Daniel was a captive there. So when Daniel prayed, God immediately sent the answer, but this prince of Persia—not visible to human eyes—temporarily stopped the angel from getting through to bring the manifestation to Daniel. But when the angel finally got through, I believe his story sounded something like this: "That pesky prince of Persia stopped me and wouldn't let me through. So for twenty-one days, I tussled with this guy, and then I whistled for Michael, the great fighting warrior angel.

Then he came and slapped him silly in a second, and I broke through, and here I am with your answer." Now, it's not written exactly that way in the Bible, but that's what it means. When Michael came, the whole thing was over, and the answer that Daniel had prayed and believed for was finally manifested.

This is a good lesson for us. The Bible says that when we pray and believe that we receive, God will send the answer. Now, it may be delayed a bit by the demonic host of the unseen realm that is over America, or wherever you live, but you can be sure that the answer will finally get through. You must understand that there is an unseen realm, and when you pray, the demonic host will try to stop the manifestation of what you prayed for from coming into the earthly realm. In Ephesians it is described this way:

> *We do not wrestle against flesh and blood, but against principalities, against powers, against the rulers of the darkness of this age, against spiritual hosts of wickedness in the heavenly places.*
> —Ephesians 6:12 NKJV

WE HAVE UNSEEN ENEMIES, AND YOU BETTER KNOW THAT THEY ARE THERE AND MUST BE DEALT WITH.

We have unseen enemies, and you better know that they are there and must be dealt with. The Bible says our battle is not with human beings but with "rulers of the darkness of this age and spiritual hosts of wickedness." Now, we can't see them, and we're not fighting with our fists, but we do have to fight them—but, thank God, He has given us some spiritual weapons to use against them.

FIGHT THE GOOD FIGHT OF FAITH

First Timothy 6:12 tells us to *"fight the good fight of faith..."* (NKJV). Whenever we pray in faith, walk in faith, or use our faith in any way, there's going to be a fight—but the Bible calls it the good fight. I like what Paul said near the end of his life:

> *I have fought the good fight, I have finished the race, I have kept the faith.*
> —2 Timothy 4:7 NKJV

What is the good fight? It is the fight of faith. We must understand that whenever we walk in faith, there will be a fight, and the fight takes time. Sometimes the answers to our prayers are slowed down because of the people factor or the enemy factor. And it is important for us to know that there is a battle going on in the unseen realm. Ephesians 6:12 lets us know that even after the death, burial, and Resurrection, there's still some wrestling and battling going on in that realm. The words in Daniel 10 let us know that there is an unseen realm...and in that realm, there's some fighting going on.

But here's the good news: Since Jesus has given us the keys to the kingdom of heaven, we have the authority to reach into that unseen realm and take hold of something in prayer. When we use those keys by believing and receiving, we're pulling what has been loosed in the heavenly realm into our realm. But you can be sure that there are all kinds of demons trying to stop it from happening. Those demons are hoping that if they put up a fight, we will just let go. But when we want our answers badly enough, we will fight the good fight of faith and hold on until we receive the expected answer.

> WHEN WE WANT OUR ANSWERS BADLY ENOUGH, WE WILL FIGHT THE GOOD FIGHT OF FAITH.

We do not want you to become lazy, but to imitate those who through faith and patience inherit what has been promised.

—Hebrews 6:12

The promises of God are inherited by faith and patience. And the same is true of believing for the answers to our prayers. Patience is just hanging on and not letting go until we see the manifestation of our prayers. And with patience and faith, we can withstand the attacks of the enemy.

When we don't see the answer to our prayers instantly, we have to keep our faith turned on and stand against the devil. The devil will do everything he can to derail your faith and patience. He will put thoughts of quitting, failure, and defeat in your mind. He will try to convince you that God doesn't love you and that He doesn't want you to have the thing you prayed for. Have you ever had those kinds of thoughts, and wondered where they came from? Well, they are straight from the pit of hell. And when those thoughts come, it's time to exert your faith and hold on until you see the answer.

WHEN WE'RE IN A SITUATION THAT CAUSES US SOME PROBLEMS, IT'S TIME TO PRAY!

Philippians gives us additional information about praying and what to do after we have prayed.

> *Do not be anxious about anything, but in every-thing, by prayer and petition, with thanksgiving, present your requests to God. And the peace of God, which transcends all understanding, will guard your hearts and your minds in Christ Jesus.*
>
> —Philippians 4:6,7

I like this section of Scripture because it doesn't leave us guessing about what we are to do. It starts out by assuring us that there is no need to be anxious or to worry about anything. Then we are instructed to pray about *everything*, which means anything that causes us to worry. So when we're in a situation that causes us some problems, it's time to pray! The verse goes on to give us another important instruction: we are to pray *with thanksgiving,* which simply means we are to thank God for what we asked for because we believe He has given it to us.

Now understand that thanksgiving is not a one-time thing we do when we pray. Thanksgiving is an ongoing process. Even though we can't see it, taste it, or hold it, when we believe that we have

THE PEACE OF GOD WILL GUARD OUR HEARTS AND MINDS.

received what we prayed for, and give thanks for it, we are not re-praying the prayer. We are just acknowledging that it's a done deal, and giving thanks to the Lord for doing it. Giving thanks is one of those things that matters even after we have prayed, and we should keep it up as long as it takes to receive the manifestation. And during that time, regardless of how long it takes, the peace of God will guard our hearts and minds. His peace will overcome every fear and worry and protect our minds. When we give thanks to the Lord and worship and magnify His name, we can just rest in God.

PRAY, GIVE THANKS, AND LEAVE THE REST TO GOD

Another important reason for praying, giving thanks, and standing strong is to defeat the enemy who tries to hold up the answers to our prayers. The Bible tells us about an incident that happened to Jehoshaphat, the king of Judah. Things had been going very well in his kingdom, and then all of a sudden he got word that three enemies were coming against him—three vast armies from three nations. And Jehoshaphat did what every one of us would have done—he got nervous. He was shaking in his boots because he knew that in the natural, he could not defeat those armies.

So again he did what we would have done—he prayed and asked God for help. And God spoke to him and said, "You know, Jehoshaphat, this particular battle is not yours, but mine, so I'd just like for you to relax and watch the salvation of your God." So Jehoshaphat received God's word by faith and said, "Cool...that's cool." Now, the Bible doesn't say it *quite* like that, but I think that's a pretty good paraphrase.

Here is the actual account as recorded in 2 Chronicles 20:

"Listen, King Jehoshaphat and all who live in Judah and Jerusalem! This is what the LORD says to you: 'Do not be afraid or discouraged because of this vast army. For the battle is not yours, but God's. Tomorrow march down against them. They will be climbing up by the Pass of Ziz, and you will find them at the end of the gorge in the Desert of Jeruel. You will not have to fight this battle. Take up your positions;

stand firm and see the deliverance the LORD will give you, O Judah and Jerusalem. Do not be afraid; do not be discouraged. Go out to face them tomorrow, and the LORD will be with you.'"

—2 Chronicles 20:15–17

So King Jehoshaphat…

…appointed men to sing to the LORD and to praise him for the splendor of his holiness as they went out at the head of the army, saying, "Give thanks to the LORD, for his love [mercy] endures forever."

—2 Chronicles 20:21

Picture this in your mind: the singers and the band are marching in front, and they're singing praises to God, giving thanks, and declaring that His mercy endures forever. The word translated as *praises* there is the Hebrew word *hallel*, which means "to rave and brag and boast about God." I like that.

WHEN THE ENEMY IS ALL AROUND US, GOD SAYS WE SHOULD PRAY, GIVE THANKS, AND LEAVE THE REST TO HIM.

It's all connected to thanksgiving and lifting up our voices. When the enemy is all around us, God says we should pray, give thanks, and leave the rest to Him. All we have to do is to continue giving thanks and singing praises to Him by raving, bragging, and boasting about Him. Now, that's a positive thing, so doing it may be out of the ordinary for some of us, because our first reaction to such a situation usually tends to be negative. But God wants to take us higher—to a place where we do what He asks us to do, thanking Him, believing Him, and praising Him because we know He will do what He said He would do!

That's exactly what King Jehoshaphat and his army did. And the Bible says as they did that, the three enemy nations turned against each other. God brought great confusion on the armies, and they ended up killing one another. And by the time the army of Israel arrived on the battlefield, the opposing armies were all dead. Jehoshaphat's army never raised a sword, but the enemy was destroyed. They did what God told them to do, and He did the rest…just like He said He would do!

What God did for them, He will do for us today. I believe that's a type and shadow for the day in which we're living. We can break things loose in that unseen realm. We can stop the devil and his demons from holding back God's answers to our prayers. We can release things and cause them to happen faster as we praise, magnify, and glorify our God. Like Moses, we can say, … *"Rise up, O LORD! Let Your enemies be scattered…"* (Numbers 10:35 NKJV). And when God is lifted up, the enemies *will* be scattered.

In the Old Covenant, when the ark was carried from one place to another, the priest walked along with the ark, which is a type and shadow of the manifested presence of God. And wherever that ark went, the enemies were totally obliterated by the presence of the Lord.

I believe that God is trying to tell us something in this day and age. We don't have to have a chip on our shoulders, hang down our heads, or let negative words come out of our mouths when things get bad. In the worst of times—when it's darker in your life than it's ever been—that's the time to lift up your voice and begin to give thanks and glorify God.

> GOD WANTS US TO PRAISE HIM WITH EVERYTHING THAT'S INSIDE OF US.

When the enemy comes against your life—or the life of someone you know and love—it's time to magnify the Lord and give Him praise and thanks. When we pray and do our part according to God's will, it causes the enemies in the unseen realm to scatter, and it brings the peace of God to protect our minds and our hearts.

God wants us to praise Him with everything that's inside of us. Instead of being negative people, He wants us to be positive people—people who give thanks and glorify our Father instead of giving up. If you are to have a fulfilling and effective prayer life, you must understand that what you do *after* you pray really does matter.

What's so difficult about rejoicing because of our God and what He's done? Whether it's answering our prayers when we pray or all the other wonderful things He's done for us, what's so tough about giving thanks? I personally believe that giving thanks to our awesome God and declaring that He is good and that His mercies endure forever is something we should do with great excitement. If we believe that He heard us when we prayed and we know that we prayed His Word, we should give thanks for those things with the assurance that they're on the way! I really do believe that the Bible teaches us to give thanks enthusiastically and joyfully, just as if we already had what we prayed for in our hands.

You'll discover later that the *Remodel Prayer Card System* cards are written in the "thank you" tense! I believe we should pray all of our prayers with thanksgiving. The wonderful thing about praying this way is that we can pray the same thing over and over for a person and not be repeating our request—we are just thanking God again and again for doing that particular thing. Praying this way took my prayer life up to another level. I agree with Dr. David Yonggi Cho, pastor of the largest church in the world, located in Seoul, South Korea, who says, "Thanksgiving is the highest form of prayer!"

THANKSGIVING IS THE HIGHEST FORM OF PRAYER!

Pastor Joe's Main Points Review

1. When we pray, we must be determined to hold on and keep believing until something happens.

2. We can only hang on until the answer comes when we learn how to give thanks, which keeps releasing our faith.

3. God often answers our prayers through people, but our prayers can also be hindered by the people factor.

4. The devil is our main hindrance, affecting the speed in which our prayers are answered.

5. We must exercise patience, which is simply staying in faith until we see the manifestation of our prayers.

7

Releasing God to Rescue Others

"And lead us not into temptation, but deliver us from the evil one."

—Matthew 6:13

As I mentioned earlier, the "R" in the R-E-M-O-D-E-L acronym stands for *rescue from evil.* Jesus came to earth to *rescue* each one of us from sin and death. The gospels speak of His explanation to the disciples that all the things they had witnessed Him doing, they would do...and even greater things than He had done on earth. Jesus is in the business of *rescuing* the oppressed, *releasing* the captive, and *setting* people free.

In what Christians refer to as the Lord's Prayer, found in Matthew 6:9–13, Jesus instructed us to pray for ourselves and other people, saying, *"Lead us not into temptation, but deliver us from the evil one"* (v. 13). There is an evil one. He is the devil. He enjoys using people to attack and come against us. He wants us to live in bondage to fear, sickness, worry, sexual sin, deception, financial concerns, dysfunctional family issues, and everything else he can think of that would hinder the progress of our spiritual walk with God, the Father and His Son, Jesus, the Christ.

On the other hand, God wants us to grow to a place where we are strong enough to overcome the evil one by using the armor of God described in Ephesians:

> *Be strong in the Lord and in his mighty power. Put on the full armor of God so that you can take your stand against the devil's schemes. For our struggle is not against flesh and blood, but against the rulers, against the authorities, against the powers of this dark world and against the spiritual forces of evil in the heavenly realms. Therefore put on the full armor of God, so that when the day of evil comes, you may be able to stand your ground, and after you have done everything, to stand.*
>
> *Stand firm then, with the belt of truth buckled around your waist, with the breastplate of righteousness in place, and with your feet fitted with the*

readiness that comes from the gospel of peace. In addition to all this, take up the shield of faith, with which you can extinguish all the flaming arrows of the evil one. Take the helmet of salvation and the sword of the Spirit, which is the word of God. And pray in the Spirit on all occasions with all kinds of prayers and requests. With this in mind, be alert and always keep on praying for all the saints.

—Ephesians 6:10–18

God wants us to become warriors who use the armor of God to conquer and overcome in every single area of our own lives and in the lives of others. Our shield of faith can become so big that when the devil's fiery darts are shot at us, every dart hits the shield, and we don't get burned because our faith puts out the fires.

YOU CAN PRAYERFULLY REMODEL SOMEONE'S LIFE

If you are anything like me, you know people who have accepted Jesus Christ as their Savior, but continue to do things that Christians shouldn't be doing. It hurts to see them getting into trouble that could have been avoided had they chosen to do the right thing and stop doing the wrong thing.

It is easy to become judgmental when we see people whose lives are out of order. But the heart of God is for us to notice these things without being judgmental and disgusted. He may even cause us to notice them, because He knows the person needs our help to prayerfully *remodel* his or her life. It is our responsibility to take what we see and pray, releasing God to move on the inside of them.

GOD WANTS HIS PEOPLE TO WALK IN TOTAL FREEDOM.

It is not our job to talk about them and what is going on in their lives to anyone other than God. We can begin by praying Matthew 6:13, asking God to *rescue* them from the evil that is attacking their lives or the evil that is attached to their lives. There is something we can do to help free them and deliver them—we can pray.

However, as we have already discovered, our prayers only have as much power as we have faith. We must believe that God wants to deliver people. If you don't believe that God wants to rescue people, you will pray halfheartedly and not much, if anything, will happen. I am convinced that God wants His people to walk in total freedom. John 10 says it best:

> *"I am the gate; whoever enters through me will be saved. He will come in and go out, and find pasture. The thief comes only to steal and kill and destroy; I have come that they may have life, and have it to the full."*
>
> —John 10:9,10

I like *The Amplified Bible* translation, which says, *I came that they may have and enjoy life, and have it in abundance (to the full, till it overflows).* Notice what is being said here. First of all, in verse 9, Jesus said He is the gate or the door. Whoever enters through Him will be saved. Over in John 14, Jesus said,

> *"I am the way and the truth and the life. No one comes to the Father except through me. If you really knew me, you would know my Father as well. From now on, you do know him and have seen him."*
>
> —John 14:6,7

JESUS IS THE DOOR

No one comes to the Father unless they go through Jesus, who described himself as "the door." Our faith in God through Jesus Christ brings eternal life, and we become children of the living God. We grow in the kingdom of God, where we live. God's kingdom becomes our home. And once we come into His kingdom, He expects us to recognize the difference between the things He does and the things the devil does. He called the devil *"the thief"* in John 10:10. He was referring to the devil and everyone who works for him, whether it is a teacher of false doctrine or someone who is taking out his anger on you. We are not at war with flesh and blood, but with the devil and his demons.

Since we know that it is the thief (devil) who steals, kills, and destroys, we must recognize that he is at work when we see friends and loved ones being attacked through sickness, disease, losing a job, financial problems, sexual sin, mental attacks, blind spots, deception, etc. God is not the author and creator of those things. He doesn't do things like that to His children. When our brothers and sisters are in prison, captured and trapped, we know the heart of God is for them to be free. Abundant life and life to the full is the opposite of stealing, killing, destroying, and being held captive in prison and bondage.

STEP OUT OF THOSE GRAVE CLOTHES!

John 11:38–44 tells how Jesus brought a dead man named Lazarus back to life. Verse 43 says, *Jesus called in a loud voice, "Lazarus, come out!"* Guess what? Lazarus came out of that grave, and when he came out, Jesus said to those who were around him, *"Take off the grave clothes and let him go"* (v. 44).

JESUS IS IN THE "SETTING FREE" BUSINESS.

Even though new believers accept Christ as their Savior, they enter the kingdom of God wearing their grave clothes. It takes a while, sometimes, for them to learn that they must resist going back to their old habits and former behaviors. We can help them shed those old rags, and one way to do it is through prayer. God says we can pray and ask Him to go into their lives and set them free. Jesus is in the "Setting Free" business. He loves to rescue and release those who are being held captive by the enemy of their souls. In Luke 4:16, we find Jesus entering a synagogue in Nazareth and standing to read.

The scroll of the prophet Isaiah was handed to him. Unrolling it, he found the place where it is written: "The Spirit of the Lord is on me, because he has anointed me to preach good news to the poor. He has sent me to proclaim freedom for the prisoners and recovery of sight for the blind, to release the oppressed, to proclaim the year of the Lord's favor."

Then he rolled up the scroll, gave it back to the attendant and sat down. The eyes of everyone in the synagogue were fastened on him, and he began by saying to them, "Today this scripture is fulfilled in your hearing."

—Luke 4:17–21

In other words, He said, "I am the guy that the Spirit of the Lord is resting upon. I am the Son of God who is anointed with the Holy Spirit and power. I am the One who is going around setting people free from the bondage of the devil." I think it is interesting that Jesus said He came to proclaim freedom for the prisoners and to set free the people who are in bondage. He said, "I came to release the oppressed." Jesus paid the price for our freedom through His death, burial, and Resurrection. His blood was required to purchase recovery of sight for those who are blind to their own sin, and it paid the price to release those who are oppressed.

In studying this in the original Greek language, I found that verse 21 is translated, *"And he began by saying to them, 'Today this scripture is fulfilled in your hearing.'"* These words are in the present infinitive tense, which means it is a continuously repeated action. So not only did Jesus say that He had come to set people free in His day and to rescue and deliver them then, but it is never going to end. It is repetitive and continuous. It doesn't begin and end there, but continues on and on. He is still in the business of setting the captives free today.

HIS MERCIES ARE NEW EVERY MORNING.

The Bible teaches that we are to pray, asking God to deliver people from their bondage no matter how they got into it. Some people are in bondage because they made a mistake or left a door open that allowed sin to enter in and disrupt everything in their lives. Yes, it's their fault, and God knows it. But His Word says that His mercies are new every morning—He *continuously* shows mercy to His children. He wants us to get out of trouble, even if we got in it by ourselves.

Included in the *Remodel Prayer Card System* is a one-sentence prayer that says, "Rescue _____ from flesh sins. Forgive him if he is sinning and break the strong-holds that keep him a prisoner to sin." Another has to do with people attacks. The prayer says, "Show _____ mercy, and open his eyes to his faults if he caused these problems." Once people are able to identify the fact that their problems are a direct result of bad choices they have made, most of them will want to stop making those bad choices. They won't want to go back to their old lives.

In the apostle Paul's second letter to Timothy, Paul was being held a prisoner in Rome. In this letter, Paul seems to know that he will soon die. It is for these reasons that he writes to Timothy. Paul not only wants to see Timothy again, but he also wants to encourage Timothy because he will have to continue Paul's missionary work after his death.

> *At my first defense, no one came to my support, but everyone deserted me. May it not be held against them. But the Lord stood at my side and gave me strength, so that through me the message might be fully proclaimed and all the Gentiles might hear it. And I was delivered from the lion's mouth. The Lord will rescue me from every evil attack and will bring me safely to his heavenly kingdom. To him be glory for ever and ever. Amen.*
>
> —2 Timothy 4:16–18

Focus on Paul's positive declaration, *The Lord will rescue me from every evil attack and will bring me safely to His heavenly kingdom. To Him be glory forever and ever. Amen.* I like that. Despite all of the negative circumstances that surrounded him, Paul chose to be a very positive guy. He knew in his heart of hearts that His Lord would rescue him from evil and give him safe passage to his heavenly home for all of eternity.

Further, he asked the Lord to have mercy on those who had deserted him and refused to stand by him in his time of need. He *chose* not to talk negatively about them. He *made a decision* not to be disgusted with them. He *opted out* of looking at them like an old house that's filled with appliances that don't work, carpet that needs to be replaced, walls that need paint, and furniture that should be thrown away…in other words, a mess.

He saw them through the eyes of an artist. He recognized their faults and knew they could be changed for the better. Yes, they were unprepared to face adversity with him at that time. They didn't have the strength to stand with him. There have been times in my life when I didn't have the strength to stand, but someone was praying and strength came. This is why we are learning to pray for people to be rescued from every evil that is attached to them or is attacking their lives. We will loose the power of God to deliver them from temptation, oppression, depression, fear, deception, and adversity.

Writing to the church in Corinth a second time, Paul said:

*Indeed, in our hearts we felt the sentence of death. But this happened that we might not rely on ourselves but on God, who raises the dead. He has delivered us from such a deadly peril, and he will deliver us. On him we have set our hope that he will continue to deliver us, **as you help us by your prayers**. Then many will give thanks on our behalf for the gracious favor granted us in answer to the prayers of many.*

—2 Corinthians 1:9–11

(emphasis added)

It is clear that we can be used by God to help people by praying that they will be delivered from every evil work, whether it is caused by people or is attached to us. Instead of becoming disgusted, frustrated, and hopeless with people, we can pray, "Lord, rescue them from the evil that has entrapped them." I am not saying this is easy to do—especially when it involves someone we love dearly, such as our mate, children, relatives, close personal friends, and others. It's tough to see them being deceived into thinking that wrong behavior is all right. It is painful to see them getting involved with people who aren't living for God. But if we don't pray, how will they ever change?

IF WE DON'T PRAY, HOW WILL THEY EVER CHANGE?

This is where the *rescue* prayer card can be helpful. Remember, this is the beginning of the *Remodel Prayer Card System*. It is so simple that you will quickly learn to think about the word *Remodel* when you're ready to pray. Then you'll automatically go through each letter of the R-E-M-O-D-E-L acronym by memory. As soon as you think of the "R," you'll think, *rescue from evil.* You will then go to the first "E" and think, *expanded love.* Then with each successive letter you will remember *more boldness, open eyes, deepen desires, extra strength,* and *Lord's will and wisdom.* You will remember everything that this acronym stands for. You will be able to pray the will of God easily and efficiently for yourself and others in a matter of moments.

This is something you can do while you are washing dishes, doing laundry, taking a shower, or driving your car. It is something you can do quickly in just a whisper. Yet it is something you can take time with when you have the time. I designed the cards so one side is the quick version and the other side is the more detailed version. So on the front of the *rescue from evil* card, there is a beautiful rescue helicopter. I chose that artwork in honor of one of the pastors on our church staff. He loves helicopters, particularly those used to rescue people.

We can pray and loose God to rescue and deliver people from the evil that is coming against them. Beneath the helicopter picture on the front side of the card is a simple prayer that says, "Father, I thank You for rescuing _____ from all evil coming against or attached to her."

When we pray this way, we are releasing God to deliver the person from evil. It is powerful! The other side of the card lists eight different categories of focused prayer. It says, "Rescue _____ from:

- adverse circumstances
- flesh sins
- people attacks
- blind spots
- mental attacks
- deception
- sickness and disease
- hurts and wounds."

There are additional specific issues described under each of those headings on the cards. Some people are held in bondage just because they are blind (not physically, but mentally and spiritually), and they don't understand or even realize that their lack of understanding or blindness is holding them in bondage. So our prayer can be, "Lord, deliver _____ from her blind spots. Rescue her and set her free in those areas."

> EVEN WHEN WE ARE WEAK, GOD IS STRONG, AND WHEN WE HOOK UP WITH HIM, WE WIN.

When the enemy attacks people's bodies with sickness and disease, we can pray for God to deliver their flesh, heal their bodies, provide a way for them to escape cancer, or rescue them from whatever physical ailment they have. Side two of each card features the detailed version of the prayer.

Now, when you don't know specifically what someone is going through, I think it is good to pray the long version—spending some time going over each area. The Holy Spirit may stir you to pray in one area a little longer than another, because He knows what the person is struggling with.

WHEN WE ARE WEAK, HE IS STRONG

So it is with many Christians. Even when we are weak, God is strong, and when we hook up with Him, we win. No matter how weak or afraid we may be, God will provide the strength and power we need to face any problem. First John 5 has a great reminder:

> *This is the confidence that we have in Him, that if we ask anything according to His will, He hears us. And if we know that He hears us, whatever we ask, we know that we have the petitions that we have asked of Him.*
>
> —1 John 5:14,15 NKJV

When we see someone struggling with illness, and they can't seem to get free, we can use the privilege God has given us to lift them up in prayer.

> *We know that **all things** work together for good to them that love God, to them who are called according to his purpose.*
>
> —Romans 8:28 KJV
> (emphasis added)

I like that—*all things!* All of us have limitations, but this verse says *all* things work for good to them that love God. Now, some people misunderstand this verse and think God causes bad things to happen to us and then brings good out of it, but that's not true. He doesn't cause bad situations, but when we find ourselves and others in trouble, God can turn it into something good and beneficial for us.

Perhaps you have been to the doctor recently and received a bad report about your health—that comes under the category of *all things.* Perhaps your daughter or son was engaged to be married, and because of problems, the engagement has been broken—their emotions are torn up and their lives are in turmoil. That is included in the *all things* category. Maybe your neighbor has lost his wife, and he is lonely and hurting…or your brother's boss chewed him out, and he is greatly disturbed by it…or you have a big bill due next week and don't have a penny in your pocket. All of these problems fall into the *all things* category.

There is no problem that we could possibly experience that isn't included in *all things.* I have discovered that no matter what I may be facing, if I give enough time to prayer, I will eventually feel a release. And when I feel that release, God always works in my behalf to solve the problem—always. It never fails. He solves the problem every time—even if I want to know something that I don't know. I have also discovered that I may pray "Rescue me, Lord," on one day, only to pick up the same thing the next day. But I have learned that I can go back and pray the "rescue" prayer each time.

God knows what you need, and He knows what you need to pray for others. He has covered all the bases, and He will not turn loose of His people. He said in His Word that He will deliver us from evil, and He will. If you, or someone you love are in a place that you don't like, pray for God to rescue you, and He will bring about something you do like!

Pastor Joe's Main Points Review

1. **When you are convinced that God wants to rescue people, you will pray wholeheartedly and release God to set them free!**

2. **You can be used by God to help people who are in bondage by praying that they will be rescued and delivered from all evil.**

3. **You have the awesome privilege of praying and releasing God to move on the inside of friends and family who are struggling in their walk as Christians.**

4. **When you commit to pray and ask God to rescue people, He is released to do so!**

8

Releasing God to Expand His Love

And this is my prayer: that your love may abound more and more in knowledge and depth of insight.

—Philippians 1:9

C ONTINUING WITH THE *REMODEL PRAYER Card System,* our focus in this chapter is on the first "E" of the *R-E-M-O-D-E-L* acronym. It stands for *expanded love.* It is clear that God's love is top priority in the Bible. God wants you and me to love one another at the highest possible level. Since each of us lives in a flesh-and-blood body that wants to do what it wants to do before considering the feelings of others, we have this little struggle going on. We often find ourselves doing things that we know do not reflect God's love. Thankfully, we can repent and tell the Lord we are sorry, and He is merciful to forgive us and wash away our selfish, often petty, and small-minded sins.

JESUS SAID, "A NEW COMMAND I GIVE YOU: LOVE ONE ANOTHER." JOHN 13:34

All of us should desire to grow to a level where we are walking in the love of God in exactly the same way that Jesus did. Most Christians know that we are commanded to love one another in the Ten Commandments (see Exodus 20). Throughout the New Testament, Jesus and Paul speak often about love. They talk about the Greek word *agape,* which is a word for love that Jesus literally coined or created.

Jesus said:

> *"A new command I give you: Love one another. As I have loved you, so you must love one another. By this all men will know that you are my disciples, if you love one another."*
>
> —John 13:34,35

He was giving the church a new commandment. Now, the Old Testament was full of all kinds of commandments, including the ten referred to earlier. But the New Testament books tell us that if we love one another as Jesus taught us to love, we will literally fulfill all the other commandments in the Bible.

He said, "Look, guys, I want you to love one another just like I love you." Then He makes this profound statement, "By this—by loving one another like I love you—all men will know that you are My disciples if you have love for one another." So Jesus said the number-one distinguishing characteristic of His followers is that we will love other Christians. He said that it is so noticeable that people looking at us from the outside will notice that we are different from anyone they have ever seen.

What is this radically different love that people will notice when they see it? What will it take for us to grow into this radical, outrageous, extravagant love for one another? I don't know about you, but I'm not sure that I have seen this kind of love. This description of love suggests to me that anyone should be able to walk into any Bible-believing Christian church in any location in the world and notice this different level of love. They should find an atmosphere that they have never witnessed anywhere else except among Christians. I don't believe the body of Christ has yet reached that goal.

I also don't believe that it is an unattainable goal, because according to the Bible, we can pray that the love of God will expand and increase inside of people. This book is all about remodeling lives through prayer. And, according to the Word of God, when people are lacking the love of God, we can literally cry out to God and ask Him to increase His love inside of them. We can ask God to cause His love to take hold of them and start controlling them.

Many people today are into remodeling older homes as opposed to building new homes or moving into a newly constructed home. When you look at an older home to buy, you are likely to see some things in that house that you are not happy with. You might be disappointed or even disgusted with all that it will take to restore that house to its original beauty and functionality. If you really like the layout of the house, the neighborhood in which it is located, the look of the house on the outside, and you're sure it has a solid foundation, you may be willing to do whatever it takes on the inside to make that house your home. But you can only make a wise decision after counting the cost.

It is exactly the same with each of us and some of the Christians we know. Our exterior may look pretty well. In other words, on the outside, we may appear to be in pretty good condition—not much remodeling work required here. But what will it take to clean up the inside in order that God's love can reside in a clean, remodeled vessel? I don't know about you but this is exciting to me. We don't have to walk away disgusted, discouraged, or bothered because someone we know (ourselves included) is not walking in the love of God at the level Jesus wants us to walk in. I know without a doubt that I can pray greater and greater amounts of the love of God into my own life and into the lives of others.

LOVE AT THE HIGHEST LEVEL

It is fascinating to learn what was going on when Jesus gave the command for us to love one another as He loves us.

It was just before the Passover Feast. Jesus knew that the time had come for him to leave this world and go to the Father. Having loved his own who were in the world, he now showed them the full extent of his love. The evening meal was being served, and the devil had already prompted Judas Iscariot, son of Simon, to betray Jesus. Jesus knew that the Father had put all things under his power, and that he had come from God and was returning to God; so he got up from the meal, took off his outer clothing, and wrapped a towel around his waist. After that, he poured water into a basin and began to wash his disciples' feet, drying them with the towel that was wrapped around him. He came to Simon Peter, who said to him, "Lord, are you going to wash my feet?" Jesus replied, "You do not realize now what I am doing, but later you will understand." "No," said

Peter, "you shall never wash my feet." Jesus answered,
"Unless I wash you, you have no part with me."

—John 13:1–8

This is love at the highest level!

In Bible days, washing feet was the job of a servant. You would either wash your own feet or a servant would wash your feet when you entered a home. But a peer or a person who held a higher social status than you would never wash your feet in those times. Jesus was considered a teacher…a rabbi, and for Him to humble himself and wash the disciples' feet absolutely blew their minds. It was a demonstration that shows us that the love of God puts other people above itself.

Jesus asked the disciples if they understood what He had done for them. Then He said:

> *"You call me 'Teacher' and 'Lord,' and rightly so,*
> *for that is what I am. Now that I, your Lord and*
> *Teacher, have washed your feet, you also should wash*
> *one another's feet. I have set you an example that*
> *you should do as I have done for you. I tell you the*
> *truth, no servant is greater than his master, nor is a*
> *messenger greater than the one who sent him. Now*
> *that you know these things, you will be blessed if you*
> *do them."*

—John 13:13–17

Jesus was saying that if we are going to love each other in the same way He loved us, we have to develop a foot-washing mentality. I like the way John describes it. Jesus said:

> *"My command is this: Love each other as I have loved you. Greater love has no one than this, that he lay down his life for his friends."*
>
> —John 15:12,13

So laying down your life simply means you put somebody else's needs above your own. Others are more important to you than you are to yourself.

I can imagine what you may be thinking, *I haven't reached this level of the love of God, Pastor Joe. I have never walked in the God-kind of love to this extent. I'd like to, but I'm not even sure I know how.* Please don't despair. We can pray more love into ourselves and into others. We can cry out to God, asking Him to increase and expand His love in each of us. We can reach the level where we are consumed with and controlled by His love.

> AS WE GROW IN THE LOVE OF GOD, THE FOOT-WASHING AND LAYING-DOWN-YOUR-LIFE MENTALITY INCREASES.

If you have children, it may not be as difficult to understand the concept of laying down our lives for our kids. If danger showed up in any form when my children were young, I always kind of pushed them behind me and positioned myself to take the blow so they didn't have to. I was laying my life down for them—making a statement that they are more important to me than I am to myself. That is a fatherly and motherly instinct that all of us have inside of us.

Well, Jesus said that we have the capability of coming to the place where we lay our lives down for one another. As we grow in the love of God, the foot-washing and laying-down-your-life mentality increases. We begin to see others as more important than ourselves. And when that happens, people are going to notice this difference in us. Especially in these days when we find so many hurried, rushed, rude, impatient people everywhere. In the stores, at the gas station, at the ballgame, literally everywhere we go, including church, we see people who are stressed out to the point that they haven't considered the feelings of others for so long, they might look at us like we're weird when we treat them nicely.

LOVE DEFINED

First Corinthians 13 is known by many as the Love Chapter. I love *The Amplified Bible* translation of these verses:

> *Love endures long and is patient and kind; love never is envious nor boils over with jealousy, is not boastful or vainglorious, does not display itself haughtily. It is not conceited (arrogant and inflated with pride); it is not rude (unmannerly) and does not act unbecomingly. Love (God's love in us) does not insist*

on its own rights or its own way, for it is not self-seeking; it is not touchy or fretful or resentful; it takes no account of the evil done to it [it pays no attention to a suffered wrong]. It does not rejoice at injustice and unrighteousness, but rejoices when right and truth prevail. Love bears up under anything and everything that comes, is ever ready to believe the best of every person, its hopes are fadeless under all circumstances, and it endures everything [without weakening].

—1 Corinthians 13:4–7 AMP

As you read those verses, you probably thought (like me), *I fall short in some of these areas.* Wow! I believe we would agree that we walk in some aspects of this, but it is a truly incredible goal. However, can you imagine what this world would be like if the people of God displayed these characteristics and started walking in an attitude that reflects a willingness to lay down our lives for others? It would look different from anything anyone has ever seen!

GOD DESIRES THAT LOVE FLOW FROM US TO OTHERS.

God wants His house—the local church—to be a display of His love. His very nature is love. He *is* love personified. God desires that love flow from us to others. When I read the Love Chapter, I can certainly identify areas in my life that require growth in showing God's love. I am sure you could grow in love, and we all know other people who need to grow in this kind of love too. The Bible teaches that we can pray and ask God to fill people with His love in abundance. We can also pray this prayer for ourselves. This is so awesome and exciting! Through prayer, we can give others, and ourselves, an extreme love makeover!

PRAY FOR EXPANDED LOVE

If you're like me and you don't particularly want to depend on someone else to pray this for you, you can pray it for yourself. This is what is so wonderful about the R-E-M-O-D-E-L acronym, I set it up so you can tell God, "I'm praying this for myself."

When we think of the first "E" in REMODEL, we can easily remember to pray, "Father, I pray for expanded and increased levels of love for _____. Release Your love in _____ and let it consume him." A Christian can read 1 Corinthians 13, known as the Love Chapter, over and over again, but I still believe it is going to take God flooding him with His love if he is going to be able to walk in it at this particular level.

How about verse 7? *Love…is ever ready to believe the best of every person.* Think about this the next time you jump to conclusions about something negative that you've heard about someone. Wouldn't it be awesome to be filled with so much love that your first thoughts would be *I know him. He would never do that. There has to be something behind it.* Wouldn't it be awesome if these were your thoughts?

Wouldn't it be terrific to wake up just bubbling over with this level of love? How about your mate? How about your Christian friends and acquaintances? You have the right to pray and ask God for this to take place in each and every one of their lives.

Paul prayed:

> *And may the Lord make you to increase and excel and overflow in love for one another and for all people, just as we also do for you, so that He may strengthen and confirm and establish your hearts faultlessly pure and unblamable in holiness in the sight of our God and Father, at the coming of our Lord Jesus Christ* (the Messiah) *with all His saints (the holy and glorified people of God)!* Amen, (so be it)!
>
> —1 Thessalonians 3:12–13 AMP

Would you like to have the love of God overflowing in your life? Wouldn't you like God's love to overflow in the life of every Christian that you come in contact with? Well, according to the Bible, we can pray this way for people. The front of the first "E" card, like all the rest, shows a simple prayer that you can memorize and pray. It simply says, "Father, I thank You that Your love is abounding in and controlling _____ in all areas of his life."

This is a perfectly scriptural prayer that you can pray for anyone, and yourself at times. The back of the card lists all the things the Bible teaches us that we can pray for Christians that will release God to move in their lives like never before. Wouldn't it be cool to go through this R-E-M-O-D-E-L acronym on your way to work in the mornings? I am convinced that God answers prayer and our prayers release Him to change people's lives.

Instead of allowing people to discourage and upset us, urging us to use our mouths to say things we shouldn't say, it would be so wonderful if we just zipped our lip and refused to say unkind things.

> PRAYER IS THE VEHICLE THAT RELEASES GOD TO MOVE IN THE EARTH.

Below is a look at some, not all, of the detailed things we can ask God to do inside others and ourselves concerning love. The *Remodel Prayer Cards* have the complete listing. The prayer begins, "Father, I thank You that Your love inside _____ is:

- ruling and uniting him in all his relationships
- being grasped by him (the width, height, and depth of Your Love)
- abounding inside him (in knowledge and depth of insight)
- guiding him when dealing with people and making decisions
- filling and controlling him."

Our prayers will release the love of God in people's lives and change them forever. Remember, prayer is the vehicle that releases God to move in the earth, and that prayer is powerful and effective in bringing change into the lives of people. If we as Christians don't operate in the authority that God has given us, we hinder the move of God on earth because we are not doing our part to facilitate God's process. We certainly are not greater than God—He is the boss and He set up the rules, which call for us to participate in His divine plan by praying that His will be done in the earth. Obviously, it is His will that we love one another with the same kind of love that Jesus had for His Father and ours. It is exciting to know that no situation is hopeless when we are faithful to do our part by praying God's will into the earth and into individual lives.

Remember what Jesus said in Luke 18:1 *"…that men always ought to pray and not lose heart"* (NKJV). This means that no matter how difficult the person or situation, we can pray and bring the kingdom of God—the presence of God—on the scene. We can pray and witness the love of God moving into the hearts and lives of those for whom we pray.

Pastor Joe's Main Points Review

1. God's love is top priority in the Bible. God wants you and me to love one another at the highest possible level.

2. When people are lacking the love of God, we can pray for them, specifically asking God to cause His love to take hold of them and start controlling them.

3. When we begin to see others as more important than ourselves, people are going to notice this difference in us. We will attract positive attention, opening a door to share God's love with them.

4. We hold the keys to release a supernatural infusion of God's love into the grumpiest, meanest, and most unloving people!

9

Releasing God to Provide a Boldness Boost

*When I called, you answered me; you made me
bold and stouthearted.*

—Psalm 138:3

HEN GOD SPOKE TO MY HEART IN
response to a plea for a tool that would
make my prayers more effective, the
R-E-M-O-D-E-L acronym came to me
almost like a bolt of lightning. Suddenly I saw that lives
could be remodeled in the same way that we remodel an
old house. It was a revelation that changed my life! We
have covered the "R," which stands for *rescuing people*

from evil and the first "E," which stands for *expanded love.* In this chapter, we will discuss the "M," which stands for *more boldness.*

This book and the *Remodel Prayer Card System* are all about praying for Christians and those who are closest to us. When we see them struggling with certain things, it is so easy to become frustrated with them. We may be tempted to talk about them, distance ourselves from them, or just throw up our hands in disgust. But God would rather that we pray for them.

God has the ability to take people who are fearful, timid, and shy, and literally drop boldness into them. In Ephesians Paul says:

> *Pray also for me, that whenever I open my mouth, words may be given me so that I will fearlessly make known the mystery of the gospel, for which I am an ambassador in chains. Pray that I may declare it fearlessly, as I should.*
>
> —Ephesians 6:19,20

If Paul, the greatest of all the apostles in the Bible, can ask others to pray for God to give him the boldness he needs to proclaim the gospel, we can pray this for each other.

Paul operated in most of the spiritual gifts which are found in 1 Corinthians 12. He was an apostle, a prophet, a teacher, a worker of miracles—he operated in the gift of healing, was able to help others, had the gift of administration, etc. He had extraordinary revelation. He was one of the top men of God of all time, and yet he asked those around him to pray for him to have boldness. That excites me and it should excite you.

EVEN IF YOU ARE QUIET AND TIMID, GOD CAN GIVE YOU MORE BOLDNESS.

If Paul experienced times when he was fearful and needed boldness, it isn't difficult to believe that it can happen to us too.

It helps me to realize that all Christians experience some fear and trepidation in our Christian walk. It doesn't mean we don't love God. It means that we lack boldness and need God to give it to us. God is the giver of boldness. And regardless of your personality, He can turn you into someone who is bold. Even if you are quiet and timid, God can give you more boldness.

I want to deal with four areas in which we need boldness if we are to be recognized as followers of Jesus who behave as He would if He were on earth today. You'll notice that there are more then four on the back of the "More Boldness" card, but four will get our point across. We need more boldness:

- in sharing our faith
- in living our faith in public

- in performing the assignments God gives us
- in standing up to the giants that we face in life.

In a later chapter, we will discuss the second "E" of the *R-E-M-O-D-E-L* acronym, which is *extra strength.* That is all about endurance. Boldness and endurance are different. *Endurance* is the ability to finish something. *Boldness* is the ability to face it. Many times we are called upon to face down some "giants" that appear in our lives…usually unexpectedly. It can be very intimidating when we see some things coming at us that we would rather avoid facing. But we can pray for God to give us boldness during these times. When you first set out to share your faith with others, you probably will need God to give you boldness.

ENDURANCE IS THE ABILITY TO FINISH SOMETHING. BOLDNESS IS THE ABILITY TO FACE IT.

BOLDNESS FOR SHARING YOUR FAITH

I have been saved for more than twenty-five years now, but the first couple of times I shared Christ with somebody, my stomach was just tied up in knots. I felt tremendous fear and anxiety. I found it to be extremely difficult to break the ice and open up to anyone about my personal relationship with the Lord. Twenty-five years later, I can tell you that I still deal with a measure of fear when I share Christ with somebody. Now, I'm not a bashful person. I can be in a crowd of complete strangers and introduce myself to everybody and get conversations going with most of them.

But there is something about telling someone about Jesus. You know the devil is going to be fighting you behind the scenes. You know that you might be rejected. The person may even talk about you and call you a religious fanatic. They may avoid you when they see you on the street or at the office. There could even be some persecution involved. Today folks are receiving warnings that their jobs could be jeopardized if they speak of Jesus to coworkers during office hours.

There is always that little barrier that we have to break through when we're sharing Christ. For me, it is not the same level of fear that I experienced as a new believer. Back then I didn't understand what I know now. I realize now that I can just whisper a prayer under my breath and ask Father God to give me the boldness to say what I need to say. Boldness has to come in an instant, because we need to move when the opportunity strikes. We have to recognize those magic moments when it is time for us to step up and say something. And you and I know there have been times when we didn't go through with it, and we have regretted the loss of that missed opportunity.

Since I started using the *Remodel Prayer Card System*, I've learned to whisper a prayer for boldness for myself and for other people. When the opportunity comes for me to share my faith, I just say, "Father, I need more boldness right now," and I trust that He is able to do it. Then I start telling the person what Jesus means to me. We don't need to tell people we're praying, and they don't have to know that we are fearful about sharing Christ. Many people have told me they experience feelings of fear when they share Christ with others. They normally are a little relieved to know that I experience the same thing myself. But I assure them that we can pray and ask God to give us more boldness. God doesn't want us to be closet Christians. He wants people to know that we are saved. He wants us to "wear" our salvation, so others might see that we are different from unsaved people.

BOLDNESS TO OVERCOME FEAR

I know it isn't easy. I wasn't always a pastor. When I was first saved and working at a secular job, I found myself in some situations that were difficult to handle. I had to make a decision whether to laugh at the perverted joke or to take some kind of stand. I had to choose whether or not to read my Bible in front of people on my lunch break. It was difficult to face the fact that my coworkers might make fun of me when I pulled out my Bible.

I had to make a decision to live righteous and not follow the crowd. It's true that fear can hold you back… fear of rejection…fear of what people are going to think and say about you. But if you are struggling with this right now, you can pray and ask God to give you more bold-ness in this area. And if you know other Christians who are struggling with it, you can ask God to give them the boldness they need, because God never intended for us to be fearful.

"DO NOT FEAR, FOR I AM WITH YOU." ISAIAH 41:10

The Bible is full of verses that tell us not to fear. I read somewhere that there are 365 "fear nots" in the Bible—one for each day of the year! I'll just give you a few to ponder that have proved to be a blessing to me.

"Do not fear, for I am with you; do not be dismayed, for I am your God. I will strengthen you and help you; I will uphold you with my righteous right hand."

—Isaiah 41:10

Fear of man will prove to be a snare, but whoever trusts in the LORD is kept safe.

—Proverbs 29:25

There is no fear in love. But perfect love drives out fear, because fear has to do with punishment. The one who fears is not made perfect in love.

—1 John 4:18

Even as a pastor, I find myself in uncomfortable circumstances when I am with people who aren't walking with the Lord. The dirty jokes fly, gossip is rampant, faultfinding and complaining are commonplace, world-weariness is evident, strained marriages have taken their toll, and problems with the kids make up almost every conversation. It is not the heart of God for His creation to be so troubled and messed up. Proverbs 28:1 says, *"The wicked man flees though no one pursues, but the righteous are as bold as a lion."*

> GOD WANTS CHRISTIANS TO BE AS BOLD AS A LION.

God wants Christians to be as bold as a lion. At the zoos I have visited, you can get really close to the lions, with just some huge boulders or chain fences between you and the lions. But I have never noticed a lion that was intimidated by me. They just act like I'm not there. If they even glance in my direction, they continue to do whatever they were doing. They are bold.

And a lion in its element fears nothing. God wants us to step up to a level of fearlessness! Part of coming to that level is praying and asking God to flood us with His boldness. God has more boldness than any of us could ever need, and He can take us from being timid to being bold in an instant. God needs every one of our personality types, but we must not allow a timid personality to be a crutch. Don't decide that you can't be bold because you're timid, shy, or quiet. Don't just assume that boldness is for those with stronger personalities than yours. You can be bold and share Christ in your own quiet way.

We can live a Christlike life in a quiet way. Boldness will come out of your personality even if you are a little bashful and easily intimidated. We don't have to scream and shout to be bold. But we must become fearless. Fear hinders, prohibits, stops us cold, causes us to back off, and gets us nowhere. When God wants us to share Christ, He will provide us with the boldness we need to speak up. We know He wants us to live in a Christlike way, and we can have all the boldness we need when we ask Him for it.

ASSIGNMENTS FROM GOD

I believe that God has a sense of humor, and I sometimes wonder if He just enjoys watching us down here, especially when He gives us an assignment. I don't know about you, but God has never given me an assignment that fell within my comfort zone. Not only that, but many times He gives me assignments that I don't even believe are within my ability zone. It

IF WE LET FEAR HOLD US BACK, WE'LL NEVER GET ANYTHING DONE.

usually involves something that I have never done, am very uncomfortable doing, and don't even feel I have the required skills to do.

When we experience a sense of urgency from God to do something that we feel completely unqualified to do, we just have no choice but to draw on God-given spiritual gifts in order to handle the assignment. If we let fear hold us back, we'll never get anything done. Let me give you a couple of examples of assignments God has given me.

God called me to pastor a church, so to prepare myself I went to Bible college. I was twenty-four years old when I graduated, and I was engaged to marry the love of my life, Gina, who I met while I was a Bible college student. I returned to my hometown, Warren, Ohio, and Gina joined me, living with my grandmother until the wedding.

Now, part of a pastor's job is to study, preach, and teach. We got everything set up to start the church, and our little team of people felt that we were ready to go, but I was a nervous wreck on the inside. And I wasn't just nervous the first Sunday—every time I preached for at least a year, I spent half the day in the bathroom with an upset stomach. I would walk out to minister and fear was all over me. My stomach was tied in knots. My whole body was in turmoil. And yet I had to do it. It was the job God had called me to do. Once I got started, the fear would gradually diminish and then leave, but the next time I was to preach, it would return.

Eventually I worked through this, but I only conquered that fear because of my prayers and the prayers of those who loved me. I found 2 Timothy 1:7, and prayed it just like it reads in the NIV version of the Bible:

For God has not given [me] a spirit of timidity, but a spirit of power, of love and of self-discipline.
—2 Timothy 1:7

Later on, I looked up that verse in *The Amplified Bible* and it says it even better:

For God did not give us a spirit of timidity (of cowardice, or craven and cringing and fawning fear), but [He has given us a spirit] of power and of love and of calm and well-balanced mind and discipline and self-control.
— 2 Timothy 1:7 AMP

That scriptural prayer gave me the boldness I needed to accomplish God's call on my life to be a pastor.

Another intimidating assignment I initially struggled with was performing weddings. When you perform a wedding, you have to read the ceremony from a book, reading a line and then looking up at the bride and groom, and then looking back down for the next line. When I first started doing weddings, I would lose my place when I looked up, and the few seconds it took to find my place made it even more difficult because I felt everyone was staring at me. I nearly fainted at the first wedding I did. I was so nervous that I didn't feel the freedom to take a breath. It was awful!

I was reading along, trying not to look up, but I just did it. I looked up at the bride and groom, and they looked back at me with genuine fear in their eyes, like they were thinking, *Oh, we're about to lose our pastor here! He's going to ruin our ceremony.* I'm not exactly sure what happened. I just kept looking up and looking down, and somehow I didn't know when to breathe. I was so nervous and tight that I began to hyperventilate! Then I finally took a big breath that everyone could hear, which caused a certain amount of embarrassment. It was just tormenting. I was so happy to have that first one over that I never wanted to do another wedding in my life.

The next one was even more difficult. It literally took five or six weddings before I was able to conquer that fear. I share this with you because I know that sometime in the near future, after you finish reading this book, God is going to give you some assignments that may be very difficult to do. You may be gripped with fear even thinking about it. And the devil—yes, there is a real devil—would love for you to back down and refuse to do what God has called you to do because of fear. We cannot give in to him and his tricks.

We must let God be in control of our lives. He does not give us assignments that we are unable or incapable of achieving. He knows better than we do that we are well able to handle anything He gives us to do. Deuteronomy 20 provides some biblical direction with regard to holy boldness:

> When you go to war against your enemies and see horses and chariots and an army greater than yours, do not be afraid of them, because the LORD your God, who brought you up out of Egypt, will be with you. When you are about to go into battle, the priest shall come forward and address the army. He shall say: "Hear, O Israel, today you are going into battle against your enemies. Do not be fainthearted or afraid; do not be terrified or give way to panic before them. For the LORD your God is the one who goes with you to fight for you against your enemies to give you the victory."
>
> —Deuteronomy 20:1–4

YOU ARE NEVER ALONE

As we pray for people to receive boldness, it is important that they also get a revelation that they will never face a challenge alone. These verses from Deuteronomy talk about going to war. We may think of battlefields and soldiers, tanks and missiles when we think of war, but there is a spiritual war going on around us all the time. The pressures are the same as if we were going into battle somewhere in the Middle East. We feel the pressure coming against us. We feel pressure about sharing Christ. We experience pressure as we attempt to live Christ in front of people who mock God and righteousness.

We feel pressure when God assigns us to do something we aren't comfortable doing. We need a revelation of the fact that God is with us and will help us to overcome what we don't have the ability to do. This is exciting! God is with us! He is as close as the mention of His name. Just as He was in the Old Testament book of Deuteronomy, He is not going to send us into any battle alone, without His help.

GOD WILL GIVE YOU THE ABILITY TO FACE WITH BOLDNESS ANY GIANT THAT COMES YOUR WAY.

Now and then some *giants* are going to pop up in our lives. Initially, we may experience fear, but God doesn't want us to dig a hole, stick our head in it, and pray for the giant to disappear. It is not going to go away! God wants us to face that giant with boldness and say, "I am going to do what the Bible says. Even though I have trouble confronting some things, I have to face down this giant. God, I ask You to give me the boldness it will take to conquer this giant of fear, and I believe You will help me." God will give you the ability to face with boldness any giant that comes your way. Fear must never stop us from doing what God has called us to do.

Now that we have covered *more boldness*, I want to describe the "M" card. On the front of the card there is a picture of a lion, along with a simple prayer that says, "Father, I thank You for flooding ____ with Holy Spirit boldness for every area of her life!"

You can commit it to memory along with the rest of the *R-E-M-O-D-E-L* acronym. When you turn the "M" card over, there is a list of seven areas, but I share four of them here, beginning with "Father, I thank You for giving ____ more Holy Spirit boldness:

- to obey and do the will of God in every circumstance
- to live Christ and righteousness in front of others
- to share Christ and His Word with others
- to stand up to the giants in her life."

For the *Remodel Prayer Card System,* I condensed the Word of God into short and simple portions that could easily be used by anyone as a tool to pray for others. But this is serious. Sometimes when things are simple, we don't take them as seriously as we should. We need to understand that when we pray God's Word from our hearts for someone to receive holy boldness, it releases Him to move. He is going to do what we asked.

It is important for us to be sensitive to the urgings of the Holy Spirit who came to live in us when we accepted

Jesus as our Savior and Lord. If He urges you to pray other things besides the words on the cards, be sensitive to pray that way. You can be as bold as a lion while remaining as gentle as a lamb. I have prayed for boldness to be increased in you as you read this book, and I conclude this chapter with a section of Scripture that I have come to love because it has increased my boldness. It is found in Romans 8:

> *We are assured and know that [God being a partner in their labor] all things work together and are [fitting into a plan] for good to and for those who love God and are called according to [His] design and purpose. What then shall we say to [all] this? If God is for us, who [can be] against us? [Who can be our foe, if God is on our side?]*
>
> —Romans 8:28,31 AMP

Be bold!

Pastor Joe's Main Points Review

1. God has the ability to take people who are fearful, timid, and shy, and literally drop boldness into them, when you pray for more boldness.

2. When you experience a sense of urgency from God to do something that you feel completely unqualified to do, you have to draw on God-given spiritual gifts and ask God for boldness!

3. Fear hinders, prohibits, and stops you cold, causing you to back off, which gets you nowhere.

4. It is important to be sensitive to the urgings of the Holy Spirit who came to live in you when you accepted Jesus as your Savior and Lord.

10

Releasing God to Open Spiritual Eyes

I keep asking that the God of our Lord Jesus Christ, the glorious Father, may give you the Spirit of wisdom and revelation, so that you may know Him better. I pray also that the eyes of your heart may be enlightened in order that you may know....

—Ephesians 1:17,18

HEN PEOPLE LOOK AT CHRISTIANS, they may see some things in our lives that are out of order. When you and I look at other Christians, we may see some things in their lives that aren't quite right, but we can pray and release God to *remodel* all of us. I have related how God supernaturally gave me the word *remodel* to help me pray more effectively for other Christians. I saw it as an acronym, adding short phrases and scriptural prayers to go with each letter.

In the previous chapters, we have covered the "R," *rescue from evil*; the first "E," *expanded love*; the "M," *more boldness*; and this chapter will focus on the "O," which stands for *open eyes*. The simplicity of the acronym is designed to introduce different prayers that we can pray and easily memorize. The prayers can be prayed for anyone and can literally change lives as you pray them.

If you have accepted Jesus Christ as your Savior, the Holy Spirit is now inside you, and it is only with His help that you can really understand the Bible. Now, I realize that an intellectual unbeliever can figure out some things by applying logic and reason to the Word of God, but they wouldn't come to the same level of understanding as a Christian whose eyes have been opened by the power of the indwelling Holy Spirit. He is the author of The Book. How wonderful to have Him alongside us to point out the real meaning of every chapter and verse in God's Word and provide revelation of those different scriptures.

First Corinthians explains that a Christian can understand the Bible by the Holy Spirit revealing it to him or her.

As it is written: "No eye has seen, no ear has heard, no mind has conceived what God has prepared for those who love him"—but God has revealed it to us by his Spirit. The Spirit searches all things, even the deep things of God. For who among men knows the thoughts of a man except the man's spirit within him? In the same way no one knows the thoughts of God except the Spirit of God. We have not received the spirit of the world but the Spirit who is from God, that we may understand what God has freely given us.

—1 Corinthians 2:9–12

All Paul was saying is this: "Hey, guys, your spirit knows what you are thinking right now. Well, it's the same with the Holy Spirit who is one with God. He knows exactly what God is thinking. It was by the inspiration of the Holy Spirit that men wrote the Bible. So don't you think the Holy Spirit knows exactly what the scriptures mean? Don't you think He can show you what He wants you to see?" The answer is, "Of course He can." Paul was praying for God to open the eyes of the Corinthian Christians so they could understand biblical principles.

I say that if Paul could pray that way for them, then we can pray that way for each other and ourselves. When Paul traveled over to Ephesus, his message was similar:

I have not stopped giving thanks for you, remembering you in my prayers. I keep asking that the God of our Lord Jesus Christ, the glorious Father, may give you the Spirit of wisdom and revelation, so that you may know him better. I pray also that the eyes of your heart may be enlightened in order that you may know the hope to which he has called you, the riches of his glorious inheritance in the saints, and his incomparably great power for us who believe.

—Ephesians 1:16–19

Notice that God has the ability to open our spiritual eyes and to let light shine into our spirit man. As that light shines in, it enlightens us and we come to know things. The word *know* in the Greek translation refers to "seeing specifics, seeing clearly, and understanding fully." So we can pray and ask God to open our spiritual eyes, as well as the spiritual eyes of others, and God will see to it that we understand biblical things as we have never understood them before.

GOD'S LIGHT OVERCOMES DARKNESS

The word *enlighten* refers to light being turned up brighter and brighter to the point that darkness begins to fade away. Let's say you were in a dark room with someone you didn't know. There was just enough light to see their shadow, but you couldn't tell who they were or whether they were a man or a woman. You wouldn't know what color their hair and eyes were. You wouldn't be able to tell what they were wearing. Then someone turns on a bright light, and all of a sudden you can make out who they are. This is often how it is with the scriptures. We can read them and even memorize them, but until enlightenment comes, we can't clearly understand them.

When we pray for God to open the spiritual eyes of our Christian brothers and sisters (and ourselves) so that we will know and understand God's Word, God turns a light on. Our spiritual eyes are opened, and all of a sudden we see details in scripture that we have never seen before. That is exciting! These days, any time I pick up my Bible to study and read, one of the first things I do is ask Father God to open my spiritual eyes. I just come out and say, "Father, I am about to read these scriptures (or I'm going to study this subject), and I ask You to open my eyes. Lord God, let me see clearly what the Holy Spirit intended when this was written. Let my mind be enlightened." All sorts of wonderful things just explode when I pray this way.

I took a day off with God recently and just spent my day studying His Word. This was not a common day, but a special day dedicated to God. I got up at 5:00 A.M., and ended up spending about fourteen hours with Him because I wanted to get some things done in the Spirit realm. I stayed with it all those hours, and it was so good. I prayed a little bit and cried out to God for some people

I had been concerned about. I did some research, looking up some key words in the Greek and Hebrew translations. I just spent the day with God. I asked Him to help me with this book. I prayed that you would understand clearly what I wanted to communicate in the book.

When I opened my Bible, I asked the Lord to make the scriptures come to life for me. I asked Him to let me see some things that I didn't currently see. It was one of the most incredible days of my life. I ended the day feeling so energized that I didn't want to sleep. I was full of God and full of life when I finished. Now, God doesn't just do this for someone like me (a pastor). God will do this for every Christian who cries out and says, "Lord, open my eyes. Cause me to see what You want me to see in Your Word." All of a sudden, a scripture that you've struggled with for years suddenly makes sense. Or you go to church and you hear the Word of God taught and it is crystal clear. You may read a book about the Bible and completely understand what it means. You "get it." I encourage you to pray this way for yourself as well as for other Christians.

Here is the attitude we need to take. Let me give you an illustration. I pray, "Lord, I am going to hold on dearly to what I believe. I am going to live and walk in what I currently know. But if there is something I am not seeing in Your Word, I ask You to open my spiritual eyes and show it to me. The minute I see it differently, I will say what I see and I will live in it." We have to have that attitude. We don't want to have a know-it-all attitude that is unteachable, but we always want to remain tender and open to all that the Lord has for us.

NEW LIGHT FOR THE DISCIPLES

Luke 24 is an interesting chapter detailing an interesting time in the history of the church. Jesus had been resurrected, and He was preparing to ascend into heaven. He knew that the disciples were frightened when they saw Him, because they had not understood when He told them before He went to the cross that they would see Him again.

> *He said to them, "Why are you troubled, and why do doubts rise in your minds? Look at my hands and my feet. It is I myself! Touch me and see; a ghost does not have flesh and bones, as you see I have."*
>
> —Luke 24:38,39

Luke goes on to describe how Jesus showed them His nail-scarred hands and feet. Then He asked them if there was anything around to eat, and they gave Him some broiled fish. He ate it in their presence. He was completely alive.

> *"This is what I told you while I was still with you: Everything must be fulfilled that is written about me in the Law of Moses, the Prophets and the Psalms."*
> *Then he opened their minds so they could understand*

the Scriptures. He told them, "This is what is written: The Christ will suffer and rise from the dead on the third day, and repentance and forgiveness of sins will be preached in his name to all nations, beginning at Jerusalem."

—Luke 24:44–47

He opened their eyes to a specific revelation of His death and Resurrection and people being saved as they believed in Him. But He had to open their eyes and their minds so they could understand what they hadn't understood all along. If God could open up the minds of His closest followers so they could understand the scriptures, then He can open your mind so you can understand them.

Never let your mouth say the words, "I read the Bible, but I can't understand it." Never let it be said of you that you are unable to interpret or understand the Word of God. Instead, let this come out of your mouth, "Father, open up my spiritual eyes so that every time I read the Bible, I understand what it is saying. Illuminate me with Your light, Lord, so that I see more clearly than I ever have and understand better than ever."

"OPEN OUR EYES, LORD"

You'll be so excited when you purchase the *Remodel prayer cards,* and you're able to pray them for others and yourself. I want to give you a taste of each card in this book, so you will realize the awesome tool that is available to you. The prayer on the front of the "O" card says, "Father, I thank You for giving ____ a greater spirit of wisdom and revelation so he can know You more intimately, and for opening and illuminating his spiritual eyes so he will fully understand all the revelations and principles of the Bible." You can pray it quickly, either from memory or with the rest of the R-E-M-O-D-E-L acronym cards. When you turn the card over, you will find a list of what I consider some of the most important revelations or principles in the Bible on one simple card. Below I've listed some of the areas found on the back of the card. The beginning prayer says, "Father, I thank You for enlightening and opening ____'s spiritual eyes so he will fully know and understand:

- Your explosive, Christ-raising power that is in him
- who he is in Christ and what Christ is in him
- what Christ has redeemed him from
- the Holy Spirit and everything connected to Him
- the power of tithing and sowing financial seed
- walking by and using his faith
- Your will and purpose for his life and heavenly future
- the holiness of God
- the fear of the Lord."

I've also included another part of Paul's Bible prayer in Ephesians, chapter one, on the "O" card. "Father, I also thank You for giving him a greater spirit of wisdom and revelation so he can know You more intimately."

What do you think? Would your life and world be changed forever if God opened your spiritual eyes to the resurrection power of Christ who lives on the inside of you? Would you agree that Christians for whom you pray, using this prayer, will begin to think, act, and live differently as they realize what explosive power is on the inside of them? They will. The Bible says faith moves mountains. If an individual's eyes are opened up to that revelation, he will begin to stand up to his adversaries. He will release the shield of faith and wield the sword of the Spirit. He will speak the Word of God with boldness. Why? Because his eyes are opened up to it. It is who he is.

Colossians 1:15 says that Jesus *is the image of the invisible God, the firstborn over all creation.* We can't see Him with our natural eyes. But God wants us to worship Him. When you study the Bible, you will find that God wants you to have an intimate, close relationship with Him. In order to do this, you need God to deposit into your spirit wisdom and revelation that open your eyes and allow you to see and understand Him. Some Christians are very awkward in their praise and worship time. They are awkward with their prayer and communication time with God.

When you see a Christian who is struggling in those areas, you can pray and ask the Lord to give him a spirit of wisdom and revelation so that he can come to know Him intimately. The heart of God is for us to know Him intimately. Some people struggle with this because they need the Holy Spirit to release more wisdom and revelation on the inside of them. We can change people who don't have a relationship with God by releasing Him to give them a spirit of wisdom and revelation. We can change people whom we love dearly or those who get on our nerves. We can look at them and see a rundown house that needs to be remodeled inside and out and start praying for change to come. You can also bring great change into the lives of your pastor or spiritual leaders by praying this prayer for them. Get ready for some awesome sermons!

> WHEN YOU CAN PRAY, THERE IS ALWAYS HOPE.

THERE IS ALWAYS HOPE

I encourage you to refuse to give up on any person or situation that looks hopeless. When you can pray, there is always hope. When we see Christians who are so carnal and messed up that we wonder if God can fix them, we must remind ourselves that He can if we'll pray. We must realize that the more they mess up, the more prayer they need. If they haven't changed and seem hopeless, it may be because we're not praying for them and releasing God to open their spiritual eyes to biblical truth. The apostle Paul prayed for believers more than anyone else. He prayed that God would be released and get involved in their lives. I believe this should motivate us to be diligent in praying more effectively so that our own lives and the lives of others can be changed.

Paul said to the church at Colossi:

> *Epaphras, who is one of you and a servant of Christ Jesus, sends greetings. He is always wrestling in prayer for you, that you may stand firm in all the will of God, mature and fully assured.*
>
> —Colossians 4:12

Paul wanted the Christians at Colossi to know that Epaphras was always praying for them. He didn't give up on them. He was a prayer warrior who wrestled in prayer, praying God's will for them consistently. He prayed first of all that they would stand firm in the will of God—that God's will for their lives would be accomplished. Then he prayed that they would mature spiritually. Think about what a blessing that must have been to those Christians— to know that someone was fervently, consistently praying God's will for their lives.

When we are faithful to take time every day to pray for the lives of individuals who seem to be out of step with God's plan, we can watch them change right before our eyes. I witnessed such a change in an individual when I attended Bible school. A friend of mine was dating a student who, although she was a Christian, seemed to have some carnal inclinations. I was concerned that she was a bad influence on my friend—that she would distract him from praying, studying, and making the most of his educational opportunity. So I began to pray—not against the girl but that the Lord would move in her life, bless her, and show her His will.

I prayed that the Lord would open her eyes, give her wisdom, and mature her in the things of God. After I had been praying for about two months, I began to notice that the girl was changing drastically. It was such a neat experience to witness the hand of God as He transformed her into a person who was intent on serving Him and doing His will. As I labored in fervent prayer, I saw her change with my own eyes, and she is still serving God today.

You can do the same thing—in fact, you should be doing it. Carnal individuals won't be praying for God to give them a spirit of wisdom and revelation. They won't be spending time praying for their spiritual eyes to be opened. That is why it is so important for us to stand in the gap for them, praying that God will bring revival in their hearts and help them to accomplish His will in their lives.

The apostle Paul prayed for the Holy Spirit to get involved in the lives of people in the church at Ephesus:

For this reason I kneel before the Father, from whom his whole family in heaven and on earth derives its name. I pray that out of his glorious riches he may strengthen you with power through his Spirit in your inner being.

—Ephesians 3:14–16

Now, if this were something that God did automatically, why would Paul pray it? If God is a sovereign God who just automatically does these things, why would He tell us to pray? If it were just automatic, we wouldn't need to pray. But Paul knew—and we now know—that whatever is loosed in heaven, we have the right and privilege to release in the lives of people here on earth so God can get in there and do something.

When we pray, using the *Remodel Prayer Card System*, we release the life-changing power of God into the lives of people He loves, and He restores them to their rightful place in Him. What a privilege and honor it is to be used in this way by almighty God.

Pastor Joe's Main Points Review

1. If you have accepted Jesus Christ as your Savior, the Holy Spirit is now inside you, and it is only with His help that you can really understand the Bible.

2. God has the ability to open your spiritual eyes and to let light shine into your spirit man when you pray and ask Him to do this for you (and others).

3. Our prayers can change people who don't have a relationship with God by releasing Him to give them a spirit of wisdom and revelation.

4. It is important for us to stand in the gap for our friends and loved ones, praying that God will bring revival in their hearts and help them to accomplish His will in their lives.

11

Releasing God to Create the "Want To"

[Not in your own strength] for it is God Who is all the while effectually at work in you [energizing and creating in you the power and desire], both to will and to work for His good pleasure and satisfaction and delight.

—Philippians 2:13 AMP

O YOU KNOW ANY COMPLACENT Christians who aren't that hungry for God? Do you have Christian friends and family members who don't desire Him more than anything on earth? Do you know people who don't love God with every fiber of their being and yet call themselves

Christians? If you do, I have written this book—and particularly, this chapter—to encourage you not to despair, because you can release God to place those desires inside of these people.

Throughout this book, I have been discussing the revelation God gave me about *Remodeling Lives through Prayer*, and how the *R-E-M-O-D-E-L* acronym was given to me as a result of crying out to God in desperation to become a more powerful and effective prayer warrior. Then came the development of the *Remodel Prayer Card System,* a simple yet effective tool that anyone can use to pray biblical prayers for themselves and others.

It can be difficult to observe the behavior of Christians who don't have the same zeal for the things of God that we have. Sometimes our frustration can escalate to the point that we become very upset with them, especially if those frustrating people happen to include our spouse, child, or parent. We may think, *I have the "want to" in me. Why don't they have it in them? I love serving God, and enjoy being involved in church. I'm living for the Lord, so why don't they? I love God with all my heart, and I want to worship Him and have an intimate relationship with Him. Why don't they want these same things?*

Why is it that some Christians remain worldly after they accept Christ as their Savior while others are noticeably changed forever? For years and years, I asked myself, and God, this question. And I'll just be completely transparent with you; I developed an attitude that was not Christlike toward people who I knew were saved but not living for the Lord. I would think, *Wouldn't it be nice if they were spiritual and hungered for God like I do? Why don't they get with it? What is wrong with them?* I looked down on them as if they were second-class Christians.

OUR DESIRE FOR GOD COMES FROM GOD

Then one day God opened my eyes to something that humbled me, and I was so ashamed and embarrassed about my bad attitude that I had to repent. I discovered that the reason I desire and love God more than anything on this planet—the reason I delight in seeking His kingdom, working for Him, and giving my life to serving Him—is because *He placed those desires inside me.* It wasn't about me. It was about the desires that God had released inside of me. I realized that there was a time in my life when I had cried out to God asking Him to place those desires in me. For all I know, God may have had other Christians praying those things into my life and

> GOD WON'T OVERRIDE YOUR WILL, BUT HE CAN CHANGE YOUR WILL.

I didn't even realize it! It is God who places in us a hunger and desire to serve Him with all of our heart, all of our mind, and all of our energies.

For years I have said that God will not bend people's will. He will not override their will and the desires of their hearts. God will not force people to do something they don't want to do. While this is true, in a way it is a half-truth. God won't force people to do something they don't want to do because He doesn't want a bunch of Christian robots running around. He wants people to desire Him and pursue Him. God won't override your will, but He can *change* your will. God can place desires inside of you that will cause you to want to do the things that He has called you to do.

The Bible relates story after story of God placing desires in people who weren't serving Him at all. One Bible story that really fascinates me—it hasn't taken place yet, but it will—is found in the book of Revelation. This is the last book in our Bible, and sometimes it is referred to as Apocalypse. In the future, there will be a person—commonly called the Antichrist—who will gain rule over most of the world. He will begin as a good person, at least on the surface, and then end up declaring that he is God and telling everyone that they must worship him.

Notice what God is able to do with the ten kings who will give allegiance to the Antichrist.

> *"The ten horns you saw are ten kings who have not yet received a kingdom, but who for one hour will receive authority as kings along with the beast [Antichrist]. They have one purpose and will give their power and authority to the beast.... For God*

*has put it into their hearts to accomplish his purpose
by agreeing to give the beast their power to rule, **until
God's words are fulfilled.***"

—Revelation 17:12,13,17
(emphasis added)

Wow! Can you imagine the leaders of ten nations giving the sovereignty of their nations over to another man? Notice that verse seventeen lets us know that God put this desire in their hearts! God has the ability to cause His purpose and will to be done by placing desires in people's hearts. My point is if God could put desires inside ten heartless, merciless kings and others, He can place them inside of you and the people you love who aren't serving God. He will not override their will, but He will *recreate* it and cause godly desires to bubble up inside them.

In Matthew 5:6, Jesus was teaching His disciples on a mountainside. He said, *"Blessed are those who hunger and thirst for righteousness, for they will be filled."* Jesus continues with this theme in Matthew 6:33, *"But seek first his kingdom and his righteousness, and all these things will be given to you as well."* God wants us to seek His kingdom more than anything else. I believe this is referring to you and me becoming involved in a church, because a local church is where the kingdom of God is manifested in the earth. God wants every Christian to be functioning in the church. He wants them to give of their time and energy to a church that is a blessing to the community in which it is located. It is central to the heart of God.

DESIRE CREATES A NEED TO SERVE

Most of us know lots of Christians who attend church, but they are not hooked up in any capacity of service. They don't seem to be interested in seeking the kingdom of God. And that's okay for a while. Sometimes you have to get a feel for what is often called "the lay of the land." This simply means that you can observe for a while, identify the needs, and offer to do your part to meet those needs.

> IF YOU LOVE GOD, THERE IS A PLACE WHERE YOU CAN SERVE HIM...JOYFULLY.

But if you have no desire to be of service in a church community, perhaps you need to ask the Lord to place a desire inside of you. When we become followers of Jesus Christ, we normally want to do everything we can to serve Him.

Now, not everyone is called to the mission field; certainly not everyone is called to pastor a church, to be an usher, greeter, worker in the children's ministry, to serve in the parking area, clean the church every week, or manage the church bookstore. The list goes on and on, but if you love God, there is a place where you can serve Him...joyfully.

If you've bought this book and read it this far, I imagine you are a person who is serving God. You have desires in you to go after God. But here's what is so exciting. You can ask God to *deepen your desire* to serve Him. You can come to a place where you want to love God more and serve Him in a greater way. And that is what the "D" of the *R-E-M-O-D-E-L* acronym is all about: Asking God to deepen the desire inside of every Christian (ourselves included) to serve Him and to long for a closer walk with Him.

I believe I have identified three things that the Lord wants us to do—three things He wants us to desire more than anything else. The first one is found in Matthew:

> *"Teacher, which is the greatest commandment in the Law?" Jesus replied: 'Love the Lord your God with all your heart and with all your soul and with all your mind.' "*
>
> —Matthew 22:36,37

It is the heart of God for us to come to a place where we love Him more than anything else on this earth.

The second one, found in Psalms, says:

> *Whom have I in heaven but you? And earth has nothing I desire besides you. My flesh and my heart may fail, but God is the strength of my heart and my portion forever.*
>
> —Psalms 73:25,26

I like that! God is my portion. He wants us to be in an intimate relationship with Him. He desires that we enjoy praising and worshiping Him and being in His presence more than we desire anything or anyone on earth!

The third thing the Lord wants from us is found in the theme scripture for this chapter, Philippians 2:13. The various Bible translations interpret Philippians 2:13 in different ways. The NIV, which I reference throughout this book and personally use more than some of the others, reminds us that *"it is God who works in you to will and to act according to his good purpose."* *The New King James Version* says God works in us for His good pleasure. *The Amplified Bible* says:

> *[Not in your own strength] for it is God Who is all the while effectually at work in you [energizing and creating in you the power and desire], both to will and to work for His good pleasure and satisfaction and delight.*
>
> —Philippians 2:13 AMP

WHEN HE MAKES US DIFFERENT ON THE INSIDE, WE'LL ACT DIFFERENT ON THE OUTSIDE.

God wants to be able to take pleasure in us and in our behavior. Our prayers release God to bring about change in our lives and in the lives of others. And when He makes

158

us different on the inside, we'll act different on the outside. Wow!

The *Holman Christian Standard Bible* (HCSB) version of Philippians 2:13 says, *For it is God who is working in you enabling you both to will and act for his good purpose.* The *Contemporary English Version* (CEV) says it this way, *God is working in you to make you willing and able to obey him.* The *New Living Translation* (NLT) says it this way, *For God is working in you, giving you the desire to obey him and the power to do what pleases him.* I really like that.

"LORD, DEEPEN OUR DESIRE TO SERVE YOU"

It is exciting for me to know that God will give me the power to love Him with all my heart, desire Him more than anything else on earth, make me willing and able to serve Him with obedience, behave and act as a Christ-follower (both privately and in the presence of others), and all I have to do is release Him through prayer to do it.

The desire to serve the Lord that you and I currently operate in was placed in us by God. So even if you love and desire Him more than anything, you can still pray for this desire to be increased and deepened. We can pray it for other Christians too. Psalm 51 was written by King David after he had sinned with Bathsheba. David was devastated and ashamed because of his actions. He felt that he had betrayed God's love for him, and he begged for God's mercy to blot out his sin. In verse 12 of the *New International Version,* he said, *Restore to me the joy of your salvation and grant me a willing spirit, to sustain me.* In *The New Living Translation,* it says, *...make me willing to obey you.* The *Contemporary English Version* says, *Make me as happy as you did when you saved me.* Awesome! When we pray for God to deepen the desire of our hearts to serve Him better and love Him more completely, without any hindrance at all, God will do it. Look what He did for David! God is no respecter of persons. David is not more important to God than you or me.

When I found all of these verses, I got an entirely different perspective about how I looked at Christians whom I might have called backslidden. In other words, they have taken a slide back to doing some things they did before Jesus came to live in their hearts. It is not our place to judge them by thinking or saying that they don't love God. That's what the devil wants us to do, but God wants us to replace our judgmental words with prayer and say, "Lord, I ask You to deepen their desires to serve You, to live for You, and to obey You."

You may be thinking, *Pastor Joe, are you telling me if I pray this prayer for every Christian, I can make them serve God?* What I am telling you is this: there may be some really hard-hearted people who don't have any desire at all to change, but you don't know who that person is on the inside. Only God knows what a person is like deep down inside. I am saying that we should never give up on any Christian, because when God is released to move inside of someone and He creates a desire and energy in them to love and serve Him, watch out! They are going to change.

I believe God wants us to pray as if it is going to happen. Too many Christians get stuck in "What if" land. Don't go there. Get stuck in "God can do all things and nothing is impossible with God" land. I urge you to pray the Word of God for people, because He can change anybody. If you believe what the Bible says—that it is God who places deepened desires in us—then it can't be hard for us to believe that God can place that deepened desire inside of another Christian.

On the front of the "D" card is the full R-E-M-O-D-E-L acronym, along with a simple prayer: "Father, I thank You for creating a deeper burning desire, to live for You and serve You, inside _____." Remember, these cards offer guidelines, but you can also pray out of your heart. God may give you some other words to pray. I call that *unction* from the Holy Spirit. You can call it whatever you want. But sometimes things just come up inside of you, and when they do, you should pray that way. The idea is to pray for God to deepen the desires in our own lives and in the lives of others. But you can pray for many things. The back of the card includes a list of what I consider to be the major biblical areas for which you would want others to have deepened desires. Let's just go through some of them so you can understand how to pray this. "Father, I thank You for creating a deeper burning desire and hunger in _____:

(As with the other prayer cards, a list follows—below are eight out of the twelve areas that all of us, as Christians, should desire.)

- to become an active member and servant in a Bible-believing church.
- to passionately follow and become a disciple of Christ
- to know Your will for her life
- to tithe and be liberal with offerings
- for You and Your Word above everything else on this earth
- for worship and spending time with You
- for the return of Christ Jesus
- for reaching lost souls."

The Bible says we should be longing and looking for Christ's return, and I have learned that we really live differently when we are doing that. You and I can pray for that desire to come into anyone. As believers, we have been given the power and authority to pray God's will into the earth. I am convinced that the prayers of faithful Christians are responsible for the changes we are seeing in people today. We must not become so complacent that we focus only on ourselves and our own walk with the Lord. It isn't that we should never do that; it's just that God wants us to be on fire for Him and praying that others will be too.

GET READY TO REAP THE HARVEST

A desire to be a "reaper" often begins with a hunger to see people accept Jesus as their Savior. Many, many Christians believe that we are living in the harvest time of the last days. If this is indeed the case, there will be so many people who are ready to accept Jesus as their Savior or to return to the relationship they once had with Him, that there may not be enough workers to lead them into the kingdom. I believe we are moving toward this time right now.

When there is a harvest out there, you and I can pray for God to send people out to reap the harvest, and He will do it. I pray for relatives, friends, and anybody who has rejected the opportunity to be born again. I pray for those who once had an intimate relationship with the Lord, but that relationship isn't the same any longer. I ask the Lord to deepen their desires to become one with Him. I pray for the Word of God to penetrate their hearts. I pray that when trouble comes to them, they will remember something they heard when they were more committed Christians than they are now. I believe God continues to answer my prayers for these dear ones, and also that He will do this for anyone who is committed to praying for their friends and loved ones to have a deepened desire to follow Him.

Pastor Joe's Main Points Review

1. It is God who places in each of us a hunger and desire to serve Him with all of our heart, all of our mind, and all of our energy.

2. Although God won't make anyone do something he or she does not want to do, He can place desires inside of them that will cause them to want to do the things that He has called them to do.

3. When we see Christian friends and family members doing ungodly things, God wants us to replace our judgmental thoughts and words with prayer, asking Him to deepen their desires to serve Him, to live for Him, and to obey Him.

4. Don't give up on the most difficult people. Don't go by what you see, keep praying that God will release His desires on the inside of them.

12

Releasing God to Provide Extra Strength

I pray that out of His glorious riches he may strengthen you with power through his Spirit in your inner being.

—Ephesians 3:16

I HAVE SHARED HOW MY FRUSTRATION concerning praying for Christians led me to ask God for a simple system with which I could pray scriptural prayers that were so easy I could even memorize them, yet containing everything people need to become all that God meant for them to be. He gave it to me through the seven-letter acronym, *R-E-M-O-D-E-L,* followed by specific phrases we can pray. After writing these on cards and adding a scripture on each card, I discovered that as I prayed this acronym, I was praying for everything the Bible teaches us we should pray for Christians! It was such a revelation and a great blessing to me that it totally altered my prayer life.

You will remember the premise of this concept having to do with remodeling a house that has old kitchen cabinets, creaky floors, undependable appliances, worn carpet and broken tile, ugly wallpaper or paneling…it's just a mess. It doesn't look good, but still it has potential. We can imagine ourselves buying the house, tearing out the floors, painting and papering the walls, installing new dry wall, new cabinets, and appliances, energy-efficient windows and doors. In other words, throwing out the old and replacing it with all things new. It's the same with believers who continue to struggle with sin.

As Christians who understand that the most important commandment God gave us in His Word is to love others as He has loved us, we must not give in to the temptation to be disgusted or disheartened by what we see among fellow believers. Instead, we have to realize that we can literally release God to change things in their lives through the vehicle of prayer. The *R-E-M-O-D-E-L* acronym is designed as a simple tool to motivate us to pray. You will recall that the "R" stands for *rescue from evil.* "E" stands for *expanded love*. "M" is for *more boldness*. "O" stands for *open eyes*. "D" is a prayer for *deepened desires*. This chapter will focus on the second "E," which stands for *extra strength*.

If you have been a Christian for a while, you are most likely attempting to do everything that you know to do to fulfill God's assignments for your life. You probably pray regularly for your family, friends, coworkers, pastor, church family, and others. Still, you may recall instances when it seemed to take much longer than you expected for God to show up. You may even remember times when you felt you were doing what God asked you to do—fulfilling your assignments—when literally all hell broke loose and things were coming at you from all sides. It can be very discouraging, and sometimes you can grow so tired and weary that you just want to quit.

The second "E" in the *Remodel Prayer Card System* and this chapter is focused on prayer for *extra strength*. It is a plea for God to flood our spirit with His strength and stamina to do what He has called us to do, to finish our assignments, to wait and not give up until our prayers are answered. This is about the ability to stay with it and not throw in the towel.

DEALING WITH THE DEVIL

We live in a cursed world. We have a devil to deal with who has never liked us since we accepted Jesus and gave our hearts to Him. He likes to win, and he knows he has lost us. He no longer has the hold on us that he once had.

THE DEVIL CAN ONLY PUSH US SO FAR BEFORE WE BUMP INTO GOD'S GOODNESS AND MERCY.

We have been translated from the devil's kingdom to God's kingdom, and the devil's only hope now is that you and I will flop and fail down here. He knows we're going to heaven, and that really, really upsets him. So the least he wants to do is to humiliate us. But he also tries to wear us down with storms, troubles, and problems—hoping that they will make us want to quit. He will put all kinds of thoughts in our minds, suggesting that God isn't going to come through, that we are not going to fulfill what God has called us to do, and that God is never going to answer our prayers. He wants us to believe that God's promises to us are not true.

It is exciting for you and me to know that the devil can only push us so far before we bump into God's goodness and mercy, which Psalm 23:6 says will follow us all the days of our lives! All we have to do is release God through prayer, and He is on the job. The Bible teaches that we can pray this for ourselves as well as for other Christians, just by whispering, "Lord, strengthen [us] them by the power of Your Holy Spirit. Give [us] them strength to do what You have called [us] them to do and never ever to quit."

I discussed the armor of God as described in Ephesians 6:10–18 in an earlier chapter. Now I will focus on the helmet section of the armor. It is called the helmet of salvation. It deals with the mind. A study of the subject in the Greek translations reveals that the helmet has to do with protecting our minds from the enemy's negative barrage of thoughts and keeping our minds focused on the outcome and seeing victory before we have actually achieved it. I don't know about you, but I still run into circumstances and situations where I grow tired even though I am wearing my helmet. There are times when I'm involved in something that is stronger than I am. You can guess what I need during those times. I need extra strength released inside of me that enables me to endure and go the distance.

Think about those Christians who don't have their helmets on. How much more do they need us to pray for them so God can release strength into their lives to help them endure and go the distance in every area?

We do not want you to become lazy, but to imitate those who through faith and patience inherit what has been promised. When God made his promise to Abraham, since there was no one greater for him to swear by, he swore by himself, saying, "I will surely bless you and give you many descendants." And so after waiting patiently, Abraham received what was promised.

—Hebrews 6:12–15

BELIEVE YOU RECEIVE IT—
AND YOU CAN HAVE IT!

When it comes to God's promises, we see in these verses that they are inherited first by faith and second by patience. Patience is simply endurance in action, and God says we can pray for people's endurance and ability to hang on when times get tough. Without endurance you may not last until God shows up with the answer.

Jesus proclaims:

> *"Therefore I tell you, whatever you ask for in prayer, believe that you have received it, and it will be yours."*
>
> —Mark 11:24

In other words, we have to believe that when we pray the will of God into the life of another person (or into our own life), God will give us what we asked for *before it shows up.* What I want you to see in this familiar verse is this: if you believe you receive it, you will have it.

Notice, however, that it doesn't mention how long it will take for us to see the answer to our prayer in a tangible way. Sometimes it takes a while. Days, weeks, months, and sometimes years pass before we literally see the answer to what we prayed for. If we don't learn to endure, we will give up. In order to stay positive and remain in what some call *staying in faith,* we have to keep thanking God that He heard us. It is imperative, however, for us to understand that the devil will take advantage of this waiting season. He will put thoughts in our minds, suggesting that we just give up and throw in the towel. This is why it is critically important for us to pray for one another, asking the Lord to strengthen us.

> *Be on your guard; stand firm in the faith; be men* [and women] *of courage; be strong. Do everything in love.*
>
> —1 Corinthians 16:13,14

The Bible makes many promises. For example, Proverbs 19:17 (NLT) says, *"If you help the poor, you are lending to the LORD—and he will repay you!"* How many of us have given to help the poor only to see needs crop up in our own lives? Is the Bible true? Will God repay you the money you gave to help the poor? I believe He will, and I believe that the above scripture, and many others like it, make that promise to all of us. But we must remember that there are no time limitations in the Spirit realm, and realize that sometimes other factors hold up our blessing and the answers to our prayers. So we must have faith and patience to endure during the waiting time. And we can pray that God's strength will enable people (including ourselves) to wait.

The verses in Hebrews 6, referred to earlier, are a perfect example of Abraham's enduring patience, especially verse

14, *"I will surely bless you and give you many descendants."* Abraham received the promise when it was given to him, but his son was not born until many, many years later. Verse 15 tells us that Abraham received what was promised after waiting patiently. Many, if not most, answers to prayer don't come overnight. You need the ability to stay with it and not quit.

EXTRA STRENGTH FOR GOD'S ASSIGNMENTS

Hebrews 12 has to do with our assignments.

> *Therefore, since we are surrounded by such a great cloud of witnesses, let us throw off everything that hinders and the sin that so easily entangles, and let us run with perseverance the race marked out for us.*
> —Hebrews 12:1

God has called everyone to do specific things for His kingdom. I'll use myself as an example. God called me to pastor Believers' Christian Fellowship in Warren, Ohio in 1982. Specifically, I was given to understand that I was to pioneer a church starting from scratch, and I have been doing that since 1983, when I actually obeyed the Lord. Then God gave me another assignment. I knew that I was to go on television, so now our services are televised. Since I have been pastoring and televising our services, lots of adversity has come my way. There have been times when I have felt like throwing in the towel just like you do with the things God has called you to do.

Let me take it to another level. Hundreds of people in the church where I pastor have been given assignments to help the church do what God has called it to do. God assigned me to pastor the church and hundreds of people were given assignments to come alongside and help. Most of these dear people responded positively to their assignments. In the performance of their assignments, like me, they have had many storms, problems, and troubles on every side to endure. I'm sure that many of them have wanted to just quit, stay home, watch television, or go out and play golf. I have found that when I pray for our church family and myself to have extra strength and endurance to continue, He provides it every time.

GOD GIVES US WHAT WE NEED TO STAY THE COURSE.

We must work hard to run our race with perseverance and endurance. We each have a race to run. It is made up of the assignments God has given us, and He doesn't want us to give up and quit. We won't finish our race in a day, nor are we likely to finish it in a month. In many cases, it takes a lifetime to complete, but God gives us what we need to stay the course. In order to do that, we must have extra strength. We need to be praying for our brothers and sisters that they will not become weary and drop out, but will continue to do what God has called them to do with patient endurance.

> *Let us fix our eyes on Jesus, the author and perfecter of our faith, who for the joy set before him endured the cross, scorning its shame, and sat down at the right hand of the throne of God. Consider him who endured such opposition from sinful men, so that you will not grow weary and lose heart.*
>
> —Hebrews 12:2,3

This is talking about the endurance Jesus needed to get through His time on earth, particularly Calvary, which was the major part of His "Project Earth" assignment. This was about Jesus finishing His race by looking past the pain and suffering of the cross to the joy that was set before Him! He was headed for Crucifixion—a slow and agonizing death.

In Luke 22:42, Jesus knelt and prayed, *"Father, if you are willing, take this cup from me; yet not my will, but yours be done."* He saw what He had to do, and asked if there was any other way to redeem mankind. But there was no other way, and He had to go through it. Where did His strength come from? God gave Him the strength, and He can give that same measure of strength to you and me. Our trials are nothing compared to what Jesus endured on our behalf.

Paul discloses in 2 Timothy 4:14–17 what he had experienced with a certain man who had caused much trouble. He said,

Alexander the metalworker did me a great deal of harm. The Lord will repay him for what he has done.
—2 Timothy 4:14

Paul was enduring severe persecution in Rome, and was probably in prison when he wrote this letter to Timothy.

You too should be on your guard against him, because he strongly opposed our message. At my first defense, no one came to my support, but everyone deserted me. May it not be held against them. But the Lord stood at my side and gave me strength, so that through me the message might be fully proclaimed and all the Gentiles might hear it.
— 2 Timothy 4:15–17

Alexander had been inciting mobs of people to persecute Paul, his Christian friends, and all of the other workers on his team. They all ran out on Paul because they didn't have the strength to endure the persecution of Alexander and his mobs. It isn't difficult to imagine how Paul felt—alone, persecuted by mobs of angry men, and his life in danger. Yet he made an incredible statement in verse 17: *The Lord stood at my side and gave me strength…* If

God could strengthen Paul in that extreme adversity, don't you believe He can strengthen you? The next time you feel like all hell has broken loose on you and your loved ones and you feel like giving up, you can pull out the second "E" in our acronym and pray, "Father, give me extra strength. Give me endurance to go the distance. Don't let me quit."

EXTRA STRENGTH TO RESIST THE TEMPTATION TO SIN

We are abundantly aware that there is sin in this world and that we still live in flesh-and-blood bodies. Certain sins can trip up some Christians more than others. In order to win in the fight to overcome sin, we really need help from heaven. The apostle Paul had started the church at Thessalonica on his second missionary journey. After teaching there for less than a month, he was forced to leave because the Jews opposed him and his teachings so strongly. On hearing from Timothy about the conditions in Thessalonica, Paul wrote this letter from Corinth, praising the Thessalonian Christians for not giving up their faith in spite of severe suffering.

First Thessalonians 3:13 is really a prayer:

> *May he strengthen your hearts so that you will be blameless and holy in the presence of our God and Father when our Lord Jesus comes with all his holy ones.*
>
> —1 Thessalonians 3:13

To be blameless and holy in God's presence, those persecuted saints had to overcome sin. In spite of everything, they had to try to live holy lives. They couldn't allow sin to trip them up. Notice Paul's words: "...strengthen them in their hearts...." We

WE CAN DO ALL THINGS THROUGH CHRIST WHO STRENGTHENS US.

can pray this prayer when we see Christians tripping up and falling into the same sin over and over again. Some Christians are backslidden—they have walked away from God. But as we discussed in the last chapter, we can ask God to deepen their desires. We also need to ask the Lord to give them spiritual endurance—strength to resist sin, say no to it, and to overcome it in their lives.

There is nothing on this earth that you and I can't overcome. Philippians 4:13 declares that we can do all things through Christ who strengthens us. The next time you see a burdened and weary Christian on the sidelines of life because they have dropped out of the race, you can pray, "Lord, flood them with extra strength and endurance so they can get back in the race and finish it." When you find yourself wanting to quit, cry out to God and ask Him to flood you with the spiritual strength and endurance you need to keep the pace as you run the race He has called you to run.

Ephesians 3:16 is our theme scripture for the second "E" of the *Remodel Prayer Card System*.

> *I pray that out of his glorious riches he may*
> *strengthen you with power through his Spirit in your*
> *inner being....*
>
> —Ephesians 3:16

I love this prayer. And by diligently praying this part of the *R-E-M-O-D-E-L* acronym, you can pray and release the Lord in the lives of people who are struggling and strengthen them in their inner man. Even while you're driving to work, taking a shower, doing dishes or housework, cutting the grass, or taking a walk, you can pray and ask God to give them endurance to go the distance as they do what He has called them to do. And God will do it. The front of the card for the second "E" has the *R-E-M-O-D-E-L* acronym on it with the "E" and the words *extra strength* in red. As you know by now, there is a simple prayer that you can memorize. The prayer on this card is, "Father, I thank You for giving _____ extra inner strength to press on and do Your will in every area of his life."

On the back of the card, there is a list of eight areas you need to cover in prayer. It goes like this: "Father, I thank You for giving _____ extra inner strength to press on and do Your will in every area of his life so he can:

- endure every test and trial
- be patient until victory and harvest come forth

- live holy and say no to sin and temptation of every kind
- finish his assignment on this earth and obey God's perfect will for his life
- fight the good fight of faith until victory comes."

I really believe that these five areas and the additional three on the card will cover everything a Christian needs to achieve strength, endurance, and victory until God's answers come.

Pastor Joe's Main Points Review

1. Every Christian needs extra strength released inside of them that enables them to endure and go the distance. We can pray for this.

2. God says we can pray for people's endurance and ability to hang on even when times get really tough.

3. When you want to quit and give up, you can ask God to flood you with the spiritual strength and endurance you need to keep the pace as you run the race He has called you to run.

4. You can pray these eight specific areas that will cover everything a Christian needs to achieve strength, endurance, and victory until God's answers come.

13

Releasing God to Reveal His Will and Wisdom

"Your kingdom come, your will be done on earth as it is in heaven."

—Matthew 6:10

If any of you lacks wisdom, he should ask God, who gives generously to all without finding fault, and it will be given to him.

—James 1:5

ARE YOU READY TO REMODEL YOUR LIFE AND the lives of those you love through the *Remodel Prayer Card System?* I pray that you are as we launch into the last letter of the *R-E-M-O-D-E-L* acronym. In this chapter, we'll discuss the "L," which stands for *Lord's will and wisdom*. Wisdom is pretty self-explanatory. God can give us wisdom so that we know what to do in every circumstance and stage of our lives. In James 1:5 we are told to ask God for wisdom, and that He will give it to us. And we can pray that for others as well.

My focus in this chapter, however, will be on the Lord's will, which is an absolutely incredible subject to study. When I was developing the cards, doing the research, and organizing the phrases and prayers that God had given me, I was amazed by the study of the Lord's will, even after being a pastor for all these years. I've prepared many messages, and some have even centered around God's will for our lives, but as I worked

WE CAN PRAY THE WILL OF GOD FROM HEAVEN INTO THE EARTH.

through the *R-E-M-O-D-E-L* acronym, I found the study of the Lord's will to be the most fascinating of all!

As we mentioned earlier in the book, Jesus provided a sample prayer in Matthew 6:9–13 that we call the Lord's Prayer. I like to look at the Lord's Prayer as an outline that gives us some different categories that we should cover when we pray.

"This, then, is how you should pray: 'Our Father in heaven, hallowed be your name, your kingdom come, your will be done on earth as it is in heaven.

Give us today our daily bread. Forgive us our debts,
as we also have forgiven our debtors. And lead us not
into temptation, but deliver us from the evil one.'"

—Matthew 6:9–13

One thing that Jesus shows us in this prayer is that we can pray the will of God from heaven into the earth. I believe He was saying that His will was already established in heaven and that it could be prayed into the earth…into people's hearts who live on the earth!

It is understood then that we can pray the will of God into the lives of other believers, with regard to what He wants them to do (their assignments) and who He created them to be. One of my favorite scriptural prayers is found in the first chapter of Colossians. I prayed it for people long before God ever gave me the *Remodel Prayer Card System.* This is the apostle Paul's third letter written from prison in Rome. Epaphras had come to Rome and told Paul that there were false teachers in Colosse who were telling the people that the Christian faith was incomplete.

They were teaching the Colossian Christians to worship angels and to follow special rules and ceremonies (see Introduction to Colossians, *New International Version*). Paul wrote to the Colossians to oppose the false teachers. He reminded them that Jesus is supreme over everything, that His death is all we need to save us from our sins, and that through Him we are free from man-made rules. Paul said:

For this reason, since the day we heard about you, we have not stopped praying for you and asking God to fill you with the knowledge of his will through all spiritual wisdom and understanding. And we pray this in order that you may live a life worthy of the Lord and may please him in every way: bearing fruit in every good work, growing in the knowledge of God, being strengthened with all power according to his glorious might so that you may have great endurance and patience, and joyfully giving thanks to the Father, who has qualified you to share in the inheritance of the saints in the kingdom of light. For he has rescued us from the dominion of darkness and brought us into the kingdom of the Son he loves, in whom we have redemption, the forgiveness of sins.
—Colossians 1:9–14

What an amazing passage of Scripture! We have been given authority to pray for the Lord's will to be done in the lives of our brothers and sisters in Christ, and to pray that He will fill them with the knowledge of His will. This is an awesome responsibility! It is something He allows us to be involved in. Remember, you can pray the REMODEL cards for yourself! It's exciting that we can also release the will of God into our lives!

GOD PLANNED YOUR ENTIRE LIFE BEFORE YOU WERE BORN.

UNDERSTANDING GOD'S WILL

When I prayed for God to show me how to help people know the will of God for their lives, I discovered two revelations that are essential if Christians are to understand God's will. The first one is that God planned your entire life before you were born, and literally wrote it down in a book that He keeps in heaven. That revelation alone will give you incredible significance, purpose, and reason for living on this planet. How amazing to realize that God himself planned your life and gave you gifts and abilities to perform the things He designed you to accomplish.

Psalm 139:15–17 clearly states:

> *You watched me as I was being formed in utter seclusion, as I was woven together in the dark of the womb. You saw me before I was born. Every day of my life was recorded in your book. Every moment was laid out before a single day had passed.*
>
> —Psalm 139:15–17 NLT

Wow! Before you and I took our first breath, God planned our lives and wrote down our days in His book. He knows what He made you to do, and He made you to do some incredibly awesome things. He created you for greatness in His kingdom. He has a plan for every person's life, and it all comes to fruition once we meet Christ.

This is so powerful!

For we are God's [own] handiwork (His workman-ship), recreated in Christ Jesus, [born anew] that we may do those good works which God predestined (planned beforehand) for us [taking paths which He prepared ahead of time], that we should walk in them [living the good life which He prearranged and made ready for us to live].

—Ephesians 2:10 AMP

This was written to Christians. God was saying that since we came to Christ, we can now fulfill what God predestined us to do.

I like the way the apostle Paul identified himself at the beginning of many books that he wrote in the Bible. To illustrate what I'm saying, Paul said in Ephesians 1:

Paul, an apostle (special messenger) of Christ Jesus (the Messiah), by the divine will (the purpose and the choice of God) to the saints (the consecrated, set-apart ones) at Ephesus who are also faithful and loyal and steadfast in Christ Jesus: May grace (God's unmerited favor) and spiritual peace [which means peace with God and harmony, unity, and undistur-bedness] be yours from God our Father and from the Lord Jesus Christ.

—Ephesians 1:1–2 AMP

In Colossians 1:1,2, Paul wrote, *Paul, an apostle of Christ Jesus by the will of God, and Timothy our brother, to the holy and faithful brothers in Christ at Colosse.* In writing to the Roman province of Galatia, Paul said in Galatians 1:1, *Paul, an apostle—sent not from men nor by man, but by Jesus Christ and God the Father, who raised him from the dead—and all the brothers with me, to the churches in Galatia.* Paul knew what he was called to do and by whom he was called. There wasn't a doubt in his mind.

ALL CHRISTIANS ARE OF SIGNIFICANT VALUE TO GOD

Every person in the body of Christ is called of God to do things. Paul identified with being an apostle, called by God to write these letters to the New Testament churches. There shouldn't be a Christian anywhere who feels insignificant. Now, living in this world with a devil that likes to place thoughts in our heads and try to tell us we are worthless and useless can be discouraging. It is so easy to think we are of no value. So many Christians struggle with rejection, and many times their struggle is legitimate. Many people today are so wounded. Some have been abandoned or abused by their own parents. Many have been told they were unwanted. Some are constantly told that they'll never amount to anything. Others are the result of rape and feel the pain of rejection.

There are all kinds of ways to enter this world and feel insignificant. You can't imagine that God could have called you to greatness, but it's important to realize that any part we play in the grand scheme of things is significant and makes us great! You can't fathom that God wrote about your life in a book. But He did, and He had a call on your life before you accepted Jesus as your Savior. You just have no capacity to fulfill your assignment until you come into Christ's kingdom. Then your spirit is recreated to do the good works that God predestined and prepared ahead of time for you to do.

HE HAS GIVEN US ASSIGNMENTS THAT ONLY WE CAN FULFILL.

God has created us with a purpose, a reason to live. He has given us assignments that only we can fulfill—things to do that nobody else can do as well as we can. There is not a Christian on this earth who doesn't have value and purpose, because God himself planned their lives. It doesn't matter who you are in the flesh. The only thing that matters is what the King and Creator of the universe decided about you. The Bible says:

God chose the weak things of the world to shame the strong. He chose the lowly things of this world and the despised things—and the things that are not—to nullify the things that are, so that no one may boast before him.

—1 Corinthians 1:27–29

GOD MAKES THINGS HAPPEN

God likes to take people from the bottom and use them for His kingdom. It blows people's minds to think that God could use common, ordinary people to accomplish uncommon, extraordinary things for Him. If God wrote something in His book that He wants you to do, and you as well as other believers are praying for His will to be done in your life, it is going to happen.

The second revelation could change your life forever. God has the ability to cause His will to come to pass anywhere, any place, at any time, in anyone—even if they don't want Him to. God has the ability to put His desires in your heart, and when He does, you will start doing what He wants done. You may not even realize it! You may think those desires are your own—that God had nothing to do with it. Wrong! I addressed this briefly in chapter 11, with regard to having a deeper desire. But let's look at another section of Scripture that brings this truth out. I can prove this theory with a scripture found in Deuteronomy.

> *But Sihon king of Heshbon refused to let us pass through. For the LORD your God had made his spirit stubborn and his heart obstinate in order to give him into your hands, as he has now done.*
>
> —Deuteronomy 2:30

This king of Heshbon was a godless leader who worshiped idols. He was not impressed with Israel or Israel's God, yet it was Israel's God who was able to make his heart stubborn and obstinate so Israel could walk in what God wanted them to walk in and do what God wanted them to do. Now, understand I am not talking about witchcraft. I don't know what God wrote in His book for me, so I am not going to pray, "Lord, do such and such"—something that I think God surely called me to do. No! I am going to pray, "Lord, whatever Your will—whatever is written in Your Word—I ask You to bring it to pass in my life." And I pray that same thing for others. I want you to see that whatever God wants to do, God can do. *He makes things happen!*

Second Chronicles 36 describes another king who didn't know God.

> *In the first year of Cyrus king of Persia, in order to fulfill the word of the LORD spoken by Jeremiah, the LORD moved the heart of Cyrus king of Persia to make a proclamation throughout his realm and to put it in writing: "This is what Cyrus king of Persia says: 'The LORD, the God of heaven, has given me all the kingdoms of the earth and he has appointed me to build a temple for him at Jerusalem in Judah. Anyone of his people among you—may the LORD his God be with him, and let him go up.'"*
>
> —2 Chronicles 36:22,23

I love this! Here is an ungodly king whose heart is moved by Israel's God to make a proclamation and put it in writing. If God could move his heart, don't you think He can put His will into your heart? Into your spouse's heart? Into your pastor's heart? Into your child's heart?

Can He put His will into my heart? I believe He absolutely can, and it is so important for us to realize that God has this ability. Remember when I said prayer is the vehicle that releases God to move in the earth? As we pray for the Lord's will to be done in people's lives, it is going to begin to take place because God is going to deposit His will in their hearts. As I shared earlier, Revelation 17 gives another example of God's will in action:

> *Then the angel said to me, "The waters you saw, where the prostitute sits, are peoples, multitudes, nations and languages. The beast and the ten horns you saw will hate the prostitute. They will bring her to ruin and leave her naked; they will eat her flesh and burn her with fire. For God has put into their hearts to accomplish his purpose by agreeing to give the beast their power to rule, until God's words are fulfilled."*
>
> —Revelation 17:15–17

The beast is the Antichrist. Remember what God did here? The Antichrist is going to rise up, and these ten kings will all be over their kingdoms. But God is going to put it in their hearts to do what He wants them to do. Think about this! First of all, God is going to put it in their hearts to give their kingdoms over to the Antichrist. He will let them think it is their own will. They will think they are doing what they want to do. He will put it in their hearts so that God's words are fulfilled. If God can put His purpose and plan into these ungodly kings who are going to serve the Antichrist, you'd better believe that God can put His will and purpose in your heart.

We need to come to a place where we are free from worrying about missing God's will in our lives. We don't need to fret about being out of God's will. When we cry out to God and ask Him to place His will in our heart, in our kids' heart, in the heart of our spouse and friends, He will do it. Jesus said we should pray that God's will be done on earth as it is heaven. So we have the right and privilege to pray the will of God into the earth.

It's also important to note that people can live and die and never fulfill the plans for their lives that were written in God's book before they were born. God has a good life all planned out for us, but He won't make us do it. But we can pray the will of God into people's hearts so that they will accomplish what God created them to accomplish. I sometimes wonder how many of us will cry tears of regret when we arrive in heaven and see what could have been accomplished in our own lives and the lives of others we care about if only we had followed God's plan. This is why it is so important that we pray for the Lord's will, as presented in the *Remodel Prayer Card System.*

"YOUR WILL BE DONE AND YOUR WISDOM COME"

The front of the "L" card contains the entire *R-E-M-O-D-E-L* acronym again: "R"—rescue from evil, "E"—expanded love, "M"—more boldness, "O"—open eyes, "D"—deepen desires, "E"—extra strength, and "L"—Lord's will and wisdom. For this card, I chose a picture of a chessboard, with the king chess piece showing, and a hand moving on a pawn. When I saw this picture, all I could think about was this card and this final letter of the acronym, because chess is a strategic game where you plan your moves three, four, or even fifteen (if you're a really good player) moves ahead. I consider myself just an average chess player, so I think ahead about two or three moves. When my opponent does something I didn't anticipate, it blows everything. But God is so incredibly smart; He knows the beginning all the way to the end. When I saw this artwork, I thought of God and His strategies. I remembered that all we have to do is simply pray, "Father, I thank You that Your will is coming to pass and Your wisdom is being deposited in _____ for every area of her life." Remember, this acronym can be memorized and prayed anywhere. You can spend as long as you want on each section of the prayer.

On the back of this card, I have listed nine detailed areas you can use as you pray for the will and wisdom of God. I've listed six of them below. The prayer starts out, "Father, I thank You that Your will is coming to pass and Your wisdom is being deposited in _____ concerning:

- the church she should become a member of and attend regularly
- her spiritual mission and purpose on this earth
- her spiritual and natural schooling and training
- all her relationships, including her marriage and children
- her occupation and dwelling place
- her financial harvest and blessing."

I believe it is important for every Christian to be a member of and attend a Bible-believing church. I don't presume to know who is to belong in what church. I would love to have some people come to my church just because I like them, but that doesn't mean they belong there. So when we pray what is listed above, we're asking the Lord to put into our hearts the church He created us to be a part of. And if you want to bless your pastor, I encourage you to pray for the spiritual mission and purpose of your pastor to be placed in his or her heart. Pastors really need God to show them every specific thing their church is to do. So pray for the will of God to be released in your pastor. Remember, you can also pray the REMODEL cards for your pastor and other ministers. You can ask God to release His will for their church and ministries into their hearts by praying this way for them!

I believe all Christians should be able to know what God has called them to do. You couldn't talk me out of the importance of this if you tried. I know what God has called me to do, and He has called you and every Christian on the face of the earth to have a place in His body…the church.

Pastor Joe's Main Points Review

1. We can pray the will of God into the lives of other believers, with regard to what He wants them to do (their assignments) and who He created them to be.

2. God himself planned your life and gave you gifts and abilities to perform the things He designed you to accomplish.

3. Every person in the body of Christ is called of God to do things. There shouldn't be a Christian anywhere who feels insignificant.

4. You can also pray God's wisdom into yourself and others! Wisdom that comes from heaven!

CONCLUSION

You Have the Tools— Now You Can Pray!

BELIEVE THE MOST EFFECTIVE WAY TO pray is to pray the known will of God or the Bible prayers that we've talked about in this book. But the Bible also teaches that Christians can pray in other tongues, and when they do, it is the Holy Spirit praying through them. Many Charismatic Christians so rely on praying in other tongues that they fail to pray the Word. My *Remodel Prayer Card System* will eliminate that lack, and will bless every Christian whether they speak in tongues or not.

If you're a Christian who does not speak in other tongues but you're interested in learning more about it, please visit my Web site, www.pastorjoe.com. My three-lesson series titled "Pentecost Power" is available to view free of charge. In this series, you'll hear about how I received the gift of tongues, what the Bible has to say about this gift, and how you can receive it yourself. After you hear the series, if you're not convinced that the gift of tongues is for you, that's okay! It is always good to listen with an open mind, but God won't force anything on any of us. Remember, whether you speak in tongues or not, the Holy Spirit is in you!

One more thing about speaking in other tongues. People who are new to our church notice that I'm not weird, yet I speak in tongues like the apostle Paul, who said, *"I thank God that I speak in tongues more than all of you"* (1 Corinthians 14:18,19). Speaking in other tongues doesn't mean you have to be weird. If someone who speaks in other tongues is weird, they were most probably that way *before* they spoke in tongues! Let's not blame that on God!

This book, however, isn't about praying in other tongues—it is about remodeling lives through praying the Word of God. As Christians, we have the awesome privilege and responsibility of praying God's will, His Word, into not only our own lives but into the lives of other people. I believe that God has given us an awesome tool in the *Remodel Prayer Card System* that we can use every day. I also believe that as you pray all the Bible prayers using this simple but effective system, your prayer life will be significantly enhanced.

YOU ARE AN IMPORTANT PART OF THE PLAN

In the "hurry-up" lifestyle of our world today, being disciplined enough to spend time in prayer every day isn't always an easy thing to do. And that's part of the beauty of the *Remodel Prayer Card System*—you can do it on the go when necessary. But you also need to have a regular prayer time, when you can spend more time remodeling lives through prayer. It helps to consider your daily schedule, and pick the time that is best for you.

For me, morning is my most productive prayer time. I'm just a morning person, so it isn't difficult for me to get up at five o'clock (yes, in the morning!) to spend some quality time with God, praising and worshiping Him and then praying that His will be done in many lives.

Whatever time you choose to pray, be forewarned that the devil will do all he can to distract you. He doesn't want you to spend time praying, particularly if you're seeing results. So you must be determined to keep your commitment, remembering that *greater is he that is in you, than he that is in the world* (1 John 4:4 KJV). God is on your side, and with His help you can do it!

> THE PRAYER OF A RIGHTEOUS MAN IS POWERFUL AND EFFECTIVE.

God has all power in heaven and in earth, but as you discovered in this book, you play a part in seeing that power released into our world. We found out it's true.

Your "asking" is an important part of the process. The Bible says the prayer of a righteous man is powerful and effective, and Jesus himself said that whatever is bound or loosed in heaven can be bound and loosed in the earth (see Matthew 16:19). So don't miss an opportunity to pray and release the powerful will of God into the lives of people in your little corner of the world.

If you're serious about having a more fruitful and enjoyable prayer life, I urge you to prioritize prayer into your daily life. Give up some television time or some book reading time and commit a portion of each day to prayer. Prayer is powerful! It is fruitful! It changes lives for eternity! It is often the difference between victory and defeat, healing and disease, and even life and death.

You now have the tools to remodel your life and the lives of others—so now it's time for you to pray!

Check out some of the many great messages from Pastor Joe.

THE RIDE OF YOUR LIFE

Your life as a Christian should be an adventurous experience. Prepare to learn about the "six" exciting rides only Christians can take!

$30 6 CD #00107
$43 6 DVD #00108

GOD GPS DIRECTIONS, DECISIONS, DESTINY

Imagine knowing exactly what direction to go, what decision to make and what your purpose is! God GPS can place your life on a new road.

$25 5 CDs #00052
$35 5 DVDs #00050

FASTING: IT'S POWER AND PURPOSE

Pastor Joe takes a fresh look at a subject as old as the Bible itself—fasting. Discover why fasting brings life-changing rewards.

$15 3 CDs #00028
$22 3 DVDs #00029

PRISON BREAK FORGIVING YOUR WAY TO FREEDOM

Unforgiveness places us into an invisible prison where God can't move in our lives. Learn how to forgive the most terrible offenses and breakout of the invisible prison!

$25 5 CDs #00055
$35 5 DVDs #00051

GOD'S OPINION ON TODAY'S HOTTEST SEX TOPICS

Sex outside of marriage, teen sex, the gay issue and even abortion are a few of the topics covered. A best seller amongst youth and adults!

$25 5 CDs #00016
$35 5 DVDs #00018

BY FAITH

Faith is a substance inside of all Christians. It can be released in five life changing ways. Learn how to change your life- By Faith!

$25 5 CDs #00025
$35 5 DVDs #00026

PENTECOST POWER: THE EXPERIENCE IS STILL AVAILABLE

Acts 2:1, 38 & 39 talk about a supernatural Holy Spirit outpouring. Pastor Joe and his family experienced this life changing power-you can too!

$15 3 CDs #00100
$22 3 DVDs #00064

PASTOR Joe

FOR MORE MESSAGE SERIES FROM PASTOR JOE GO TO
WWW.PASTORJOE.COM

Never Again Wonder How to Pray for Christians...
Use the Simple REMODEL Prayer Card System!

Prayer is the vehicle that releases God to move on this Earth! That's why I've created the Remodel Prayer Card System to allow you to pray all the New Testament prayers in as little as ten minutes a day! Watch your own life and others you care for be changed – from the inside out. Using the simple acronym, REMODEL, you'll never need to fret or become unsatisfied with the spiritual or natural condition of anyone again. Watch your prayer life become revolutionized and the people you love changed forever as you use the "Extreme Makeover Prayer System." Order yours today!

YOU'LL DISCOVER:
- How to rescue people from evil

- How to pray for God's love to fill and direct the lives of others

- How to pray for God to fill people with boldness

- How to release God to open spiritual eyes for Bible revelation

- How to pray for backslidden Christians - helping them come back to God

- How to pray God's will and purpose into the lives of others

Plus much more!

$8.00 Each set   #00013

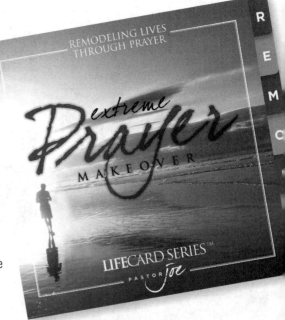

To order by phone, using your MasterCard, VISA, American Express or Discover credit card
call 1-877-330-3341 or visit www.pastorjoe.com

WWW.PASTORJOE.COM

ABOUT THE AUTHOR

OE CAMENETI IS THE SENIOR PASTOR OF Believers' Christian Fellowship, located in his hometown, Warren, Ohio. Joe and his wife, Gina, pioneered BCF in 1983 after graduating from Bible school. In addition to pastoring a large church, Joe hosts a weekly teaching program called, "Pastor Joe," which airs on his Web site, www.pastorjoe.com as well as on television. God has gifted Pastor Joe with a unique teaching gift that makes the Bible practical, relevant, and easy to understand. Every time you hear him teach, you will walk away knowing how to implement the Word of God into your daily life, enabling you to grow spiritually and to know God better. Joe and Gina Cameneti are the parents of four children, Joseph Jr., David, Michele, and Deanna.

TO CONTACT THE AUTHOR
Joseph Cameneti Ministries
Believers' Christian Fellowship
P.O. Box 1949
Warren, OH 44482
1.877.330.3341
Web site: www.pastorjoe.com

Please include your testimony of help received from this book when you write. Your prayer requests are welcome.